Giving Voice to the Silent Pulpit

Giving Voice to the Silent Pulpit

A Layman Explores the Differences between
Popular and Academic Christianity

BARRY E. BLOOD SR.

RESOURCE *Publications* · Eugene, Oregon

GIVING VOICE TO THE SILENT PULPIT
A Layman Explores the Differences between Popular and Academic
Christianity

Excerpts from the article "Preachers Who Are Not Believers" by
Daniel Dennett and Linda LaScola. Copyright © 2010. Used with
permission of the authors.

Poem: "Church Concerns" by James S. C. McIntosh. Used with
permission of the author.

Resource Publications
An Imprint of Wipf and Stock Publishers
199 W. 8th Ave., Suite 3
Eugene, OR 97401

www.wipfandstock.com

ISBN 13: 978-1-61097-298-7

Manufactured in the U.S.A.

Church Concerns

Some mainline churches
Are shrinking their display,
As elderly members
Slowly fade away.

A dearth of young families
With new ideas bold
Have needs not being touched
By these churches of old.

The causes of the malady
Are hard to determine.
Is it clergy, congregation,
Theology, or sermon?

There are many excuses
Like "its happening overall."
Still the church's future should not be ignored
Until the danger of its fall.

Open discussion should be the first step
In finding a solution.
"Heads in the sand"
Only leads to continued delusion.

—James S. C. McIntosh

Contents

Preface / ix

Acknowledgments / xiii

1 A New Understanding / 1

2 Does It Matter What We Believe? / 15

3 Ten Doctrines / 19

4 Take a Deep Breath . . . / 62

5 Questioning Our Imagination / 66

6 Coming Clean / 74

7 A New Concept of God / 78

8 Be Honest with Yourself / 82

9 With Knowledge Comes Change / 85

Bibliography / 95

Preface

G ROWING UP in a small mid-west town in the 1950s was, perhaps, the best time and place to grow up . . . ever. I'm quite sure I didn't feel that way then, but now, looking back it seems so clear. Life at that time in our country's history seemed to be more simple, safe and tranquil.

Much of community life, in those days, revolved around the church. What was considered "regular" church service in those days consisted of: Sunday morning worship, Sunday evening worship and youth group meeting, and Wednesday evening worship. Most churches also sponsored some sort of Cub Scout, Boy Scout, Brownie, or Girl Scout Troop. Then there were men's and women's groups and a multitude of other ad hoc groups involved in an assortment of projects. Most every citizen of every community was, at one time or another, involved directly or indirectly in one or many of these activities. It was the American way of life in small town USA. I grew up in that environment . . . and enjoyed every minute of it.

The First Methodist Church at the corner of West and Emerson Street became my "home" church. In addition to the regular church activities I was involved in our Boy Scout Troop, which met there on Monday evenings. On most meeting nights, several of us boys would arrive early so we would have time for "horseplay" before the Scout Master arrived. One of our favorite activities was to play hide and seek inside the church. With free run of the building we found some really out of the way hiding places! To this day I believe I know several nooks and crannies in that church building of which even the custodian is unaware.

I was not a religious fanatic by any means, but the church and all that it represented, was very important to me in my formative years—as it was, I believe, for most young people of that era. As I grew into adulthood, I began to take on, what I considered to be, my share of responsibilities in the church. I served as an usher, sang in the choir, and served on various boards and committees. At one point I became trained as a lay minister and served as a substitute preacher from time to time. I guess I would be called an active Christian.

However, in 1993, at age fifty-seven, my understanding of the Christian belief system began to change. This change was prompted by a life altering experience, which is revealed in chapter 1 of this book. The change was not something that happened overnight; rather, it took several years of study and investigation—years during which I found myself hoping I was wrong about what I was discovering. But in the end I realized I was not wrong. Today I am still a Christian, but a Christian with a much deeper and more honest and mature understanding of what Christianity is about. A great deal of what I mean by "a much more honest and mature understanding" will be dealt with, in detail, in the following chapters.

I anticipate that this book will, to a degree, cause you, the reader, some of the same pain and stress that I felt in the early stages of my investigation and discovery. Do not despair. In the end, I am convinced you will become aware of a much richer and far more rewarding understanding of the Christian faith, than you have ever before experienced.

In my opinion, if the Christian church is to live on, as a force for good in human society, the greater depth of knowledge that is exposed herein, will of necessity, become the norm in Christian education among the laity.

Please remember as you read . . . this is not a book in which I make known my *opinion* on religious teachings. Rather it is a book in which I *report*, with straightforward honesty, information about Christianity and Christian doctrine that is unknown to a vast majority of the laymen and laywomen of the faith.

I will be reporting the results of many years of study. Some of my findings will certainly invade the reader's comfort zone. For this, I make no apology. Knowledge can sometimes be painful, but ignorance also has a price. I will not maliciously tear down sacred beliefs. I will merely report what the past two and one-half centuries of Biblical scholarship has revealed and how it has changed the church's understanding of Christian doctrine.

The church has a responsibility to keep the laity informed of new knowledge, but has chosen not to do so. Instead, the church has, more often than not, chosen to deny, rebuff, or simply remain silent about new knowledge that would counter ancient beliefs. Today the gap between what is preached from the pulpit and what the clergy and hierarchy of the church know has become problematical.

This problem can only be solved by exposing the church's hidden secrets. To my way of thinking, there is no choice—the church must turn to a more honest doctrine or perish. Perhaps together you and I can start to solve this problem. This book is my attempt to get that ball rolling.

BEB

Acknowledgments

I WISH to express appreciation to two groups of free thinking and questioning Christians who, like me, have struggled for the past several years to understand the Christian
faith in an honest and mature manner, consistent with the
intellectual worldview of the twenty-first century. The first
group, known as the Sojourners, is made up of both retired
pastors and Christian laypersons and has been together for
the better part of four decades. Though there has been turn-
over in members and leaders through the years, their bent
toward an informed study of the Bible and the Christian
faith has never wavered. This group has been my primary
support for discussion and debate on myriad controversial
topics. The second group, also a study group, has no official
name. I suppose they could be described affectionately as,
"Wally's group." It too is composed of pastors and laypersons. They meet weekly for discussion and study of current
events and the application of Christian principles in our
daily lives. Both these groups have helped me sustain my
desire to complete this book.

I also wish to thank my lovely wife, Christine, for
putting up with my compulsive study of religion during
the early years of my investigation. I believe the word she
used most frequently to describe my compulsiveness was
"obsession." Never the less, she challenged me in ways
that, many times, required me to dig deeper to validate my

information, and thus often led me to a clearer understanding of my position.

Last, but perhaps most importantly, I wish to thank and praise my copyeditor, United Church of Christ minister Lenni Lissberger. Her insight and editing skills have been invaluable. She offered experienced guidance throughout the writing and editing phases of my manuscript. Without her assistance this book might never have seen the light of day!

1

A New Understanding

THE DISCOVERY

FOR THE past eighteen years I have been on a quest for a better understanding of gods and goddesses, religion in general, and Christianity in particular. What I have discovered during this search is sometimes shocking, sometimes exciting, always interesting.

I was prompted to begin this study as a result of an incident that took place in 1993. After thirty years of service in the management ranks of a major Aerospace company, I had retired, at age fifty-five. A year later, I was working as a consultant for a software company with offices overlooking Tampa Bay, on Florida's west coast.

On Thursday, January twenty-eighth, at approximately one o'clock in the afternoon, I left our offices on the eleventh floor and made my way to a small café on the first floor of that same building. As I stood there in the food line, waiting to be served, I heard a "popping" noise behind me. It sounded like a balloon bursting. Then another and another.

I turned in the direction of the noise and suddenly realized there was a man just six feet from me with a pistol in his outstretched hand, firing at people as they sat eating their lunch. Along with the other patrons of the café, I dove for the floor. Lying there I listened to the shots being fired . . . seven . . . eight . . . nine. With each shot I felt certain the next bullet would be for me . . . ten . . . eleven. It is odd the thoughts that come to you at such a time as that. I remember thinking, "I hope he shoots me in the head so I won't have to lie here in pain." Then the firing stopped. The shooter laid his weapon on a table and walked out. I was alive, but just six feet away, three young men lay dead, two women wounded.

My life had been spared.

In the days and weeks that followed, friends and family members would say things like, "God must have other plans for you," or, "There was a guardian angel on your shoulder that day." Statements that I myself had said to others in the past—normal Christian thoughts and expressions of concern.

But for some reason, this time they struck me as odd. Maybe it was because this time the statements were directed at me.

I began to have questions, "If God had something else in mind for me, does that mean he had nothing else in mind for those three young men who died, all of whom had a wife and small children?"

"If there was a guardian angel on my shoulder that day, why was there no guardian angel on their shoulders as well? Why?" These were not frivolous thoughts, they bothered me greatly.

I spoke to my pastor about these lingering questions, but there seemed to be no satisfying answer. Real questions, but only (what seemed to me) evasive answers.

Then another question began to creep into my mind. "Who was really in charge that day?" "Who was really making the decisions about who would live and who would die? Was it the God I had been taught to worship and pray to all my life, or was it Paul Calden, the man with the gun?"

I had been a Christian all my life. I had read the Bible since I was a kid. I was active in my church: an officer, elder, teacher, lay minister, and a believer. But something just wasn't adding up this time. I wanted to know more. More about God, more about his omnipresence, his omnipotence, and his omnificence. And what about free will? Can we just do what we want, to whom we want, whenever we want, and God in his ever presence, all powerfulness and all knowingness will just let it happen? How does that mesh with the idea of a loving and caring God of all? I needed more than I was ever going to get from studying the gospels year after year in an adult Sunday school class.

Thus began a study that, as of this writing, has lasted eighteen years and is continuing. During this time I have read more than two hundred and fifty books on these subjects. I have interviewed dozens of pastors, bishops, religious scholars, and professors of religion. I have attended numerous seminars, lectures, and pastoral workshops regarding Christianity and other religious matters.

The study has pulled me in many directions. I am certain now, however, I have a much better understanding of what God is and is not, and what religion is and is not.

Once one delves deeply into the history of gods, goddesses and religion, it becomes clear that the average person lives in a delusional cocoon regarding such subjects. Very few people take the time or effort required to study or inform themselves about the origins or nature of religions. Some are encouraged not to ask questions about such things, for others it is simply enough to believe what they were taught in childhood or in a Sunday school class.

For Christianity this has resulted in the formation, over the past three hundred years, of two distinct belief systems; one which I will call "Popular Christianity" (the domain of the people in the pews), and the other, "Academic Christianity" (the domain of the church professionals from the pulpit upward).

These two belief systems (Popular vs. Academic) are so different in their respective views of Christianity that if stripped of their Christian identity and viewed separately, most people would not recognize them as elements of the same religion.

The church hierarchy is aware of this duality. It is discussed at seminars and workshops. Students are taught in our seminaries that this situation exists. But it is seldom even hinted at from the pulpit.

When I first discovered this "Popular vs. Academic" aspect of the Christian faith, I became quite angry. Why were we, the people in the pews, not aware of the Academic side of Christianity? Why were we still being taught and spoken to as if we were children?

I was angry, resentful, and embarrassed at having been (in my opinion) made a fool of by the very people I had looked to all my life for spiritual guidance.

My anger led me to search even deeper into what I then considered a web of deceit. I sought out both active and retired pastors and spoke to them about what I had discovered. Their responses confirmed my studies. Of the more than twenty pastors I interviewed, only one stood firm in his defense of the Popular doctrine of the church. The others quite freely admitted there is a great disparity between what is preached from the pulpit and what is understood by the professionals of the church.

For several months I became a dropout. I stopped attending church, period. When friends asked why, I was reluctant to explain, I needed time to sort through my own thoughts before I attempted to explain this confusion to others. Why was the church perpetrating such a charade? How could so many millions, even billions, of people be kept in the dark for so long? Were my findings wrong? What could possibly motivate the church to withhold such vital information?

After a time of personal reflection and contemplation, however, I came to the conclusion I still needed the church. We human beings are social animals, and the church was, for me, a place of socialization. If it were dishonest in its teachings, I would attempt to rectify that situation in whatever small way I could.

THE DECEPTION

The information I will share with you is known by most all religious leaders. It is taught in most seminaries and college courses on religion.

This information is not something I take lightly, nor is it something I have simply made up. *I can say with confidence that what I am about to share with you is the very fabric of Academic Christianity.*

You may ask, "Why have I not heard of this before?" As you read, the reason should become somewhat obvious. The church is not eager for you to ask questions that would require answers that refute thousands of years of religious teachings.

For the past three hundred years, the church (in this case I mean the hierarchy, from the local pastor to the national and international leaders of institutional Christianity) has known a version of Christian doctrine that is quite different from the doctrine preached from the pulpit. Most all Christian professionals have expanded their understanding of God and Jesus far beyond the images they learned as children. Yet they have not informed the laity, you and me, so that we might follow along this broader, more mature path as well.

It is as though an invisible velvet curtain hangs between the pulpit and the pews, a curtain preventing the people in the pews from growing into mature Christians, a curtain separating intellectual honesty from myth and folklore.

The Reverend Dr. Jack Good, retired pastor with forty years service to the United Church of Christ, describes this separation in his book, *The Dishonest Church*.[1]

> Pastors and other trained professionals of the church often have developed a system of beliefs that is qualitatively different from the faith they

---

1. Good, *The Dishonest Church,* 9.

communicate to local congregations. Their individual faith has developed, in most cases, after an intense and sometimes painful time of questioning and dismantling, and reconstruction. For reasons that are not clear, these leaders assume that local church members are either unwilling or unable to survive a similar process. So in an act of dishonesty that threatens to erode the core of the church's mission, they hold one kind of faith for themselves while the literature they produce for the laity and the sermons they deliver assume another, basically different, style of faith for the non-professional.

Such pretext has gone undetected for most of the past three hundred years. But as the educational level of the average individual continues to rise around the world, more and more people are seeing through and around the invisible velvet curtain, to the detriment of the church. In this, the information age, it is becoming harder and harder for the church to keep the laity in a state of religious ignorance.

As a result, this deception is having a devastating effect on the church. Beginning around 1960, mainline Christian churches started to see a decline in membership, which is continuing today. During this same period, evangelical and fundamental churches saw an increase in members. Now, however, even the evangelicals and fundamentalists have begun to slip.[2]

There are many reasons for this decline in membership, but one reason that is of increasing concern—and the one I am personally most concerned about—is the

2. National Council of Churches, 2009 Yearbook.

intellectual dishonesty that continues to spew forth from the church in its literature, its liturgy, its sermons and its day-to-day contact with the people in the pews.

In 2010 the journal, *Evolutionary Psychology* published an article titled, "Preachers who are not believers."[3] The article was the report of a study made possible by a grant from a small foundation, administered through Tufts University. The study was conducted by Linda LaScola, a clinical social worker with years of professional experience as a qualitative researcher and psychotherapist, and philosopher Daniel Dennett, the author of *Breaking the Spell* (2006).

The abstract of the study states the researchers' belief that: "There are systemic features of contemporary Christianity that create an almost invisible class of non-believing clergy, ensnared in their ministries by a web of obligations, constraints, comforts, and community." The study then sets out to answer the question: "Are there clergy who don't believe in God?"

For the study the researchers identified five brave pastors, all still actively engaged with parishes, who were prepared to tell their stories. All five were Protestants, with master's level seminary education. Three represented liberal denominations and two came from more conservative, evangelical traditions.

Here are excerpts from two of the interviews.

Darryl, a thirty-six-year-old Presbyterian minister with a church outside of Baltimore wrote:

3. Dennett and LaScola, "Preachers," 120–150.

> I am interested in this study because I have
> regular contact in my circle of colleagues—both
> ecumenical and Presbyterian—who are also
> more progressive-minded than the "party line"
> of the denomination. We are not "un-believers"
> in our own minds—but would not withstand
> a strict "litmus test" should we be subjected to
> one. I want to see this new movement within the
> church given validity in some way. I reject the
> virgin birth. I reject substitutionary atonement.
> I reject the divinity of Jesus. I reject heaven and
> hell in the traditional sense, and I am not alone.

Adam, a forty-three-year-old worship minister and
church administrator in a large Church of Christ congregation in South Carolina, although raised Presbyterian,
became involved with conservative Christianity. Even in
seminary, when confronted with questions and contradictions in the study of academic Christianity, he stayed fo-
cused on his desire to help people live a Christian life that
would ultimately lead them to eternal life.

Today, however, he struggles through his job, hiding
his true beliefs:

> Here's how I'm handling my job on Sunday
> mornings: I see it as play acting. I kind of see my-
> self as taking on a role of a believer in a worship
> service, and performing. Because I know what to
> say. I know how to pray publicly. I can lead sing-
> ing. I love singing. I don't believe what I'm saying
> anymore in some of these songs. But I see it as
> taking on the role and performing. Maybe that's
> what it takes for me to get myself through this,
> but that's what I'm doing.

He'd like to get out of this situation, but hasn't yet figured out how to do it:

> I'm where I am because I need the job. Still, if I had an alternative, a comfortable paying job, something I was interested in doing, and a move that wouldn't destroy my family, that's where I'd go. Because I do feel kind of hypocritical. It used to be the word "hypocritical" was like a sin. I don't hold that view anymore: there is goodness, and there is sinfulness; it's one or the other. It's black or white. That there's ultimate absolute truths that are mandated in scripture or given by a supernatural being. I don't see those anymore, so I use the word "hypocritical" differently, as in, I'm just not being forthright. But, at the same time, I'm in the situation I'm in, and rationally thinking about it is what I've got to do right now.

He considers himself an "atheistic agnostic" and wonders how non-believers fill the void left by loss of faith, or even if they feel a loss. For his part, he says:

> I've got to the point where I can't find meaning in something that I don't think is real anymore. I guess mostly inside I do toy with the fact that, "OK, what's driving me to get up every morning?" I used to be very devotional-minded. Get up, and maybe read a passage of scripture; say a prayer; ask God to guide me through the day, totally believing that he would. Now it's like, "You don't have that." So there's a lack of guidance. But at the same time I find it more free, where I create my own day.

When researchers asked one of the other pastors they talked with if he thought clergy with his views were rare in the church, he responded, "Oh no, you can't go through seminary and come out believing in God!" Surely an over-statement, but a telling one. As Wes put it:

> . . . there are a lot of clergy out there who—if you were to ask them—if you were to list the five things that you think may be the most central beliefs of Christianity, they would reject every one of them.

In their concluding statements the researchers made this observation:

> These are brave individuals who are still trying to figure out how to live with the decisions they made many years ago, when they decided, full of devotion and hope, to give their lives to a God they no longer find by their sides. We hope that by telling their stories we will help them and others find more wholehearted ways of doing the good they set out to do. Perhaps the best thing their congregations can do to help them is to respect their unspoken vows of secrecy, and allow them to carry on unchallenged; or perhaps this is a short-sighted response, ultimately just perpetuating the tightly interlocking system that maintains the gulf of systematic hypocrisy between clergy and laity.

My opinion, of course, is that the unchallenged secrecy is one of the primary reasons for the decline of the church.

WHY IS THIS SO?

One might assume that of all human institutions, those of a religious nature would be among the most honest. My studies have shown: that assumption would be wrong.

Let me share with you four reasons why this deception continues unabated;

First, the people in the pews are so indoctrinated with the "Once upon a time" religious stories of their youth they expect to hear nothing else from their minister. Therefore local ministers, in order to keep their jobs, continue to preach the "ole time religion." It becomes a matter of self-preservation.

Second, pastors/ministers/priests, in spite of their own personal college and seminary "awakening," do not feel the laity is capable of understanding or accepting the more intellectually honest and mature version of religious doctrine.

Third, the clergy have not been trained to help others make the transition from ancient doctrine to a more progressive understanding, so even if they wanted to, most are unprepared to lead their congregation across such an awesome divide.

Fourth, religious (church) officials often forbid clergy to preach or speak in ways that would expose ancient church doctrine to question. They fear the truth would cause the laity to feel resentment for past misinformation and leave the church, thereby negatively affecting membership, power and (most importantly) revenue.

Perhaps there are other reasons as well, but these are the ones most spoken and written about by religious scholars.

WHY I AM WRITING

The church, in its unfortunate attempt to stand solidly behind a worldview that no longer exists, has rendered much
of its doctrine and dogma nonsensical and irrelevant.

My purpose is not to add to the demise of the church.
On the contrary, my purpose is to,

1. make the Christian faith, once again, a relevant part of
   the intellectual society,

2. make the Christian faith something that will appeal to
   educated and uneducated alike,

3. make Christianity a religion that does not ask its adherents to believe folklore and myth as fact, and

4. make Christianity a religion that does not ask its adherents to leave their brains at home when they come
   to church on Sunday morning.

I believe there is a great need for religious community—a place where people who value compassion, toler-
ance, justice, and inclusiveness can come together to plan
and celebrate and work for the common good of all; a place
where people of all generations, present and future, can be
taught the teachings of Jesus. But before that can happen,
the church must admit to its past misinterpretation and
misrepresentation of much of the scripture and its outdated
doctrine and creeds.

Later in this book I will explain several items of dogma
or doctrine, which need to be reinterpreted and expressed
in more intellectually honest terms. I will not waste time
"candy coating" my comments. I suspect I will be more

direct than some would like, but I do not want anyone to misunderstand what I am saying.

I will not engage in wishful thinking or suppositions. What I relate to you will not be only my impressions or my opinion (unless noted as such), rather, I will explain to you what the professionals at the academic level of Christianity (clergy, church hierarchy, professors of religion, etc.) are teaching and writing about Christianity in the twenty-first century.

2

Does It Matter What We Believe?

IN THE early 1990s the movie, *A Few Good Men,* starring Tom Cruise and Jack Nickleson was playing in theaters. In one courtroom scene, Nickleson was on the witness stand being interrogated by Cruise who pointed his finger at Nickleson, and in a loud voice demanded, *"I want the truth!"* Nickleson's face turned red, the veins in his neck bulged, and in an angry voice he replied, *"You can't handle the truth!"*

For the past three hundred plus years, the professionals of Christianity (clergy, theologians, biblical scholars, professors of religion, hierarchy of the church) have, in essence, spoken this same line to the people in the pews, regarding the truth of religion. They have, by their actions, said over and over, *"You can't handle the truth"*—about God, the Trinity, prayer, the virgin birth, the resurrection, original sin, atonement, heaven, hell, and eternity.

For more than three hundred years, the professionals of Christianity (with only a few exceptions) have chosen to remain silent about the true history and authenticity of God, religion, and other doctrines of the church. They have opted instead to allow the myth of an immature belief system to continue unabated, maintaining an "our father who art in heaven" theology.

But now, at the beginning of the twenty-first century, intelligence is beginning to overtake the silence of the church. More than just a few of the church professionals are breaking rank. They are talking and writing about a true understanding of gods and goddesses, religion, and faith. Their words are sometimes shocking to those who have never been exposed to a true critical examination of the faith, however, such information is not new, it has simply been suppressed.

Some, who would squelch this new truth, object to its publication on the grounds that the people in the pews should believe whatever they want to believe. If the old belief system gives them comfort, leave it alone. After all, many of them "*can't handle the truth!*"

My question is this. Does it matter? Does it make one "hoot" of difference what the masses believe? Should we who profess a more mature and intelligent understanding of religion, just remain silent? Or, does it matter?

As you might guess, yes, I think it does matter.

It is a well-known fact that what people believe will affect how they act.

- If one believes there is a supernatural being, "up there" or "out there" that will hear and answer prayer, it lessens one's feeling of personal responsibility. "I will pray for the hungry and the homeless, and *God* will care for them."

- If one believes that his or her sacred scripture contains the inerrant word of God and the moral law(s) for all time, then all debate over moral issues is dead. The holy book will tell us who to love, who to hate, who to trust . . . and who to kill.

- If one believes sacred scripture contains the inerrant word of God, one might be persuaded to strap on a vest full of explosives, walk into a crowd of innocent people and blow oneself up.

- If one believes sacred scripture contains the inerrant word of God, one might feel justified in dropping "smart" bombs on those considered to be the enemy.

- If one believes a holy book contains the inerrant word of God, one might feel compelled to bomb an abortion clinic, kill an abortion doctor, or suggest "taking out" the leader of a foreign country.

Belief in a god and/or an ancient book is a belief based on delusion. Twenty-first-century knowledge explains where those gods and goddesses and those ancient books came from and renders such belief systems impotent. Facts, evidence, reason, and just a little bit of logic must prevail if the human race is to mature beyond its current state.

Yes, I know all the arguments about leaving room for the spiritual and the transcendent and not wanting to disturb the comfort zone of the people in the pews—but such "right brain (emotional) thinking" is hastening the demise of Christianity and bringing the world closer and closer to the brink of disaster.

It is time for Christianity—and for that matter all religions—to become honest, and first of all, to become honest with themselves. If (and only if) the religions of the world can rise above the ancient mythology and superstition of the past and begin to forge a more intellectually honest understanding of the human condition, will there be hope for the future of our world and the church; a future that will find justice, inclusiveness, and peace for all.

I write because I firmly believe the emphasis on forging this more intellectually honest doctrine must begin with the laity of the church. The professionals and academies have already shown they are unwilling or afraid to make the first move. It will take, in my opinion, a critical mass of laymen and laywomen urging the clergy to speak out in honesty, if Christianity is to make this much needed transformation. But even before this can happen, the laity must become informed, and that is what this book is all about. It is my attempt to expose the differences between what the people in the pews have been taught and the more mature understanding of Christianity that lives in our universities and seminaries.

What we believe does matter, it shapes the very way we live our lives.

3

Ten Doctrines

INTELLECTUAL HONESTY requires the church to tear down the invisible velvet curtain hanging between the people and the pulpit. It requires the church to face the consequences of decades of preaching and teaching doctrine that was known to be outdated or just plain false.

There will be pain and anger involved. Many devout Christians will feel betrayed, and some will leave the church in despair. The church will struggle to survive in the wake of criticism and rejection, but in truth, it is already struggling because the advance of knowledge is slowly eroding the effectiveness of the invisible curtain.

Much of this problem could have been avoided had the church been wise enough to advance or revise its own doctrine each time science made new discoveries regarding nature, the cosmos, or the human condition; beginning with the works of Copernicus, Galileo, Newton, and others; continuing down to the present. Instead, in my opinion, paranoia and fear of losing control prevailed, and the authority of church doctrine began to split with reality.

Today the gap between doctrine and reality can no longer be hidden. Almost weekly there is a new book released—authored by a bishop, priest, minister, religious scholar, or college professor—denouncing some element of doctrine or exposing the fallacy of yet another religious belief.

In April 2010, Rev. Gretta Vosper, chairperson and founder of The Canadian Center for Progressive Christianity and author of the provocative, best selling book, *With or Without God: Why the Way We Live Is More Important Than What We Believe*, made this statement while speaking to a gathering of clergy at the Common Dreams 2 Conference, in Melbourne, AU:

> We can no longer assume we are the most informed people in the room. Those who had previously believed that everything said from the pulpit was factually true, have, for the last many years, been demanding answers to questions we could easily avoid in the past. Those outside the church, who had all found it too crazy to believe in the first place, have felt hugely vindicated by what they see as us being caught with our pants down or, perhaps more accurately, that, all this time, we have had no clothes on at all and masked that with the bright colors of our vestments and the gilded beauty of our edifices.

There appears to be at least ten major differences between the thinking of those who profess a belief in popular Christianity and those who have reached a more educated and mature understanding, which scholars call academic Christianity. I have listed these ten differences below. Each item begins with a short side-by-side description of the doctrine under discussion, followed by an account that represents current scholastic understanding of the subject.

The descriptions and accounts are merely representations. There are likely hundreds of variations of each entry, related to denominational differences, Bible references, or personal interpretations. Nevertheless, the depiction listed here will allow the reader to observe the dissimilarities.

THE CONCEPT OF GOD

Popular Christianity (as understood by the people in the pews)	Academic Christianity (taught in our colleges and seminaries)
God is a supernatural being, "up there" or "out there" that knows all, sees all, and is ever present. He listens to and answers prayers and from time to time intervenes in the world to impose his will and/or perform miracles.	Spirits and gods have existed over the past thirty to forty thousand years of human evolution. They are creations of the ancient mind, a human construct, used to explain the forces of nature, to provide security and to give credence to the moral rules of the group (tribe, village, nation, etc.).

One hundred thousand. That is the estimated number of gods and goddesses that humankind has invented or imagined over the past thirty to forty thousand years. One hundred thousand, more or less, gods and goddesses of various descriptions and powers who exhibited control over the elements of nature and the lives of human beings. One can verify this fact in just about any book on the history of gods and goddesses.

The earliest of these were not the sort of gods we often think of today. They were, rather, the spirits of the forces of nature. Our early forefathers believed that the wind and the thunder, the sun and the rain all had a mind of their own and came and went as they pleased. They had no other way of explaining or understanding these phenomena; our forefathers believed that if they pleased these spirits the spirits might look favorably upon them. So began the practice of worship and praise and sacrifice. These first objects of human worship were not thought of as gods that controlled the wind and thunder, etc., they were the wind and thunder, etc. This form of belief is referred to as Animism.

Another of the earliest objects of worship was the totem. Totems were a form of good luck charm for the group or tribe. A totem might be an animal, a tree or plant, a certain rock or carving. These objects, if small and portable, were often carried on a hunt, or into battle with a neighboring tribe. The totem provided protection and good fortune.

Among scholars and historians there is debate as to whether spirits or totems came first. Most likely they co-existed over several thousand years. Totems, of course, still exist in our society today in the form of sports teams and school mascots. The Chicago Bears, the Denver Broncos, the Princeton Tigers, the Los Angles Rams are all current manifestations of the ancient totem.

The next significant change came thousands of years later and involves ancestral worship, more specifically, worship of deceased ancestors. These alleged spirits of the dead were worshiped as gods. In fact, there are stories of the ritual eating of the flesh and drinking of the blood of ancestors to acquire their special skills or knowledge. These actions or rituals are the precedents of our present day communion or Eucharist rituals.

Ancestral worship occurred at two levels of the society. Each family, of course, had its own ancestors, whom they worshiped. Additionally, the ancestors of the leader of the group or tribe became the gods of the social unit (the tribe, the gathering, the region, etc.).

Most groups continued to worship the spirit gods of nature in addition to their ancestral gods. This led to the belief of multiple deities (known as polytheism), usually assembled into a pantheon (group) of gods and goddesses, along with their own mythologies and rituals. Polytheism was the typical form of religion during the Bronze Age and Iron Age.

The period from about eight thousand years BCE to nearly one thousand BCE, saw yet another change in worship patterns. During this time period, groups invented (and that is truly the appropriate word) gods who were in charge of other gods: super-gods, "most high-gods," gods in the manner of Zeus of the Greeks, Osiris of the Egyptians, or Marduk, the Babylonian god. Many religions were formed in this manner, called henotheism. Henotheism is the worship of many gods or goddesses with one supreme god held as the ruler over other lesser gods, and with each god or goddess having his or her own powers and skills. Other religions—including the early Hebrew religion— recognized the existence of other gods but worshiped only one. This form of worship is called monolatry.

Then came a period when humankind made a great shift in its belief systems. This period began around the beginning of the third millennium BCE and continued for more than two thousand years. It was a shift from a belief in many gods to a belief in either one god—called monotheism—or to no god at all, as in the case of Buddhism and Jainism. This became known as the "Axial Period" because of the magnitude of the shift in the belief systems of so many of the world's people.

However, in spite of this shift to monotheism, religions in the form of polytheism, and henotheism still represent much of the world. Even today, except for the Abrahamic religions—Christianity, Judaism, and Islam—most of the world's religions are overwhelmingly polytheistic. For example, Hinduism, Mahayana Buddhism, Confucianism, Taoism and Shintoism in the East and tribal religions in Africa and South America are mostly polytheistic and are widely practiced and remain very popular in their ancestral areas.

It is relatively easy for us, today, to agree that the many gods of the polytheistic era—the pre Axial era if you will—were the product of human imagination. Isis, Marduk, Zeus, Athena, and the gods of the sun, rain, thunder, fertility, and all the rest, were products of the human quest for an explanation of the world around them. Gods are a byproduct of the ability of mankind to imagine abstract beings and give them not only a life of their own but also all manner of shape and size. New gods were formed when a group of people sufficiently convinced themselves of the need for a deity to serve them in a particular manner. After deriving an image of the new god or goddess and assigning him or her the needed powers, the group developed rituals and ceremonies of worship that were sure to placate the new god and assure his or her protection or good will. Such gods or goddesses were normally local in nature, belonging to a certain tribe, nation or region.

What we tend to lose sight of is the fact that the God of the monotheistic religions of today, which includes Christianity, Judaism, and Islam, is simply a refinement of the man-made gods of the polytheistic and henotheistic age.

I know the reader probably doesn't want to hear that, but if you truly want to understand religion, you must allow yourself to absorb the historical fact that the monotheistic God is just as much a part of the human imagination as the polytheistic and henotheistic gods were a part of the human imagination.

For centuries the Jewish, Christian, and Islamic religions wrapped themselves in the idea that the God of Abraham was different. He had "revealed" himself to mankind. This claim had the supposed authority of freeing the Abrahamic God from the accusations of being a god of human construct—an imaginary god. The doctrine of "divine revelation" was used to defend their unique understandings of the Abrahamic God. The Jews proclaimed that God revealed himself and his will to Moses through the Torah. Christians proclaimed that God revealed himself and his will through Jesus of Nazareth. Muslims proclaimed that God revealed his will to Muhammad through the angel Gabriel. The Mormons proclaimed that God revealed himself to Joseph Smith through the angel Moroni.

But in recent history, notably the last two or three hundred years of religious scholarship, the doctrine of divine revelation has been mostly abandoned by religious leaders. Intellectual honesty makes revelation an almost embarrassing scheme. And so, the term God—with a capital "G"—has become understood in the postmodern academic world, to be just as much a human creation as were the gods of the pre-Axial world.

All talk of God or of the gods, is human talk. The description of God as a supernatural being, "up there" or "out there" watching over his creation, listening to prayers, and from time to time intervening in the world to impose his will, is a figment of the human imagination.

Before we go any further, let the meaning of that statement sink in—the description of the God of the Abrahamic religions, Judaism, Christianity, and Islam, like every other supernatural god, is unquestionably a figment of the human imagination. You can deny it, you can argue about it, you can debate it, you can refuse to believe it, but you cannot change the historical facts. All gods and goddesses of all times are the product of the human mind.

But don't just take my word for it, read a couple of books on the history of religions or the origins of the god concept—there are dozens of them in your library—and you'll begin to understand there is a great difference between learning about gods and goddesses from within the cocoon of religion, and studying the same subjects from outside those biased walls. Perhaps four of the best books on these subjects, in my opinion are: *The Evolution of the Idea of God* by Grant Allen, *The Golden Bough* by Sir James George Frazer, *A History of God* by Karen Armstrong, and *The Evolution of God* by Robert Wright.

Now, did I just imply that I do not believe in God? What I said was, the description of God found in the Torah, the Bible, and the Quran, which portrays God as a "being," is nothing more than human construct. If there is anything that can be called "God," it is not the supernatural being found in the holy books of the Abrahamic or any other religions. That description worked for the ancient world, but it is a bankrupt concept in the worldview of the twenty-first century.

～

If the Christian Church is to be honest with its adherents it must explain—in unambiguous terms—that the God described as a supernatural "being" is purely mythological. Anything less than a full disclosure of this fact will only add to the confusion and prolong the dishonest nature of the pulpit/people relationship. If people want to believe in a god in the sky, or fairies, or Santa Claus, or any other make-believe character, let it be known for what it is, human imagination.

～

THE BIBLE AS THE "WORD OF GOD"

Popular Christianity (as understood by the people in the pews)	Academic Christianity (taught in our colleges and seminaries)
The scriptures, i.e. the Bible, both the Old and New Testaments, are the literal or inspired word of God and are the revelation of God to man. They are the infallible, authoritative rule of faith and conduct.	The Bible is not considered a collection of factual statements written, dictated, or otherwise inspired by God, but instead, it is a collection of books written by many human authors that document the authors' beliefs and feelings about God *at the time of its writing*—within a specific historic/cultural context.

The Pew Research Center continues to report that as many as 78 percent of Americans believe that the Bible is the "word of God." And many of them believe it is the "literal" word of God.[1]

Bishop John Shelby Spong, retired Bishop of the Newark Diocese of the Episcopal Church, is fond of relating the story of a time when he was debating a Baptist minister who made the statement that the Bible was "the infallible and inerrant word of God." To which Bishop Spong replied, "Have you ever read it?"

If one has just a small understanding of the history of religion and the ethnic epics of the ancient world, they would be embarrassed at such an idea. The Bible is a compilation of stories that make up the epic story of the Hebrew people and reflect their way of relating to the world around them.

Creation stories can be found among nearly every ethnic group and every religion on earth and each of them is different. The stories are a way to explain that which was, for them, unexplainable. They come in a multitude of varieties and forms. Many contain great detail and exciting adventure, but in the final analysis they must be understood for what they are—attempts to explain the unexplainable.

The two versions of the Hebrew creation story found in the first two chapters of Genesis form the basis for the Judeo-Christian religion. The stories probably traveled by oral transmission for centuries before being written down for the first time. The story in the second chapter was written around 950 BCE. The other version—in the first chapter—came into existence about a hundred years later. There are many contradictions between the two. We won't go into

1. Pew Survey, *Religion and Politics*, Sec. IV.

those contradictions in this book nor will we talk about the unknown authors of these two stories. Those details can be found in the book by Richard Elliott Friedman titled, *Who Wrote the Bible.*

The writings of the Bible reflect the thinking of many authors, each writing at a different time, to a different group of people, for a different reason. The Old Testament was written over a period of approximately 800 years and echoes the worldview of the Hebrew people during several differing periods of their nation's development. The New Testament, written between 50 CE and 125 CE reflects the early development stages of the Christian church.

There are many good books in print today that explain the origin and purpose served by the writers of these documents. The idea that they were somehow written or inspired by a god is, of course, ludicrous when one begins to understand the origin of the gods, as we have previously discussed.

The "inerrancy" theory is, in fact, a relatively new idea that began about one hundred fifty years ago with the writings of Princeton theologian Charles Hodge. In his book, *Systematic Theology,* Hodge asserts that the Bible's moral and religious truths and its statements of fact are all inspired. In a sermon given at Princeton in 1866 Hodge stated, "The Scriptures of the Old and New Testaments are the Word of God, written under the inspiration of the Holy Spirit, and are therefore infallible, and of divine authority in all things pertaining to faith and practice, and consequently free from all error whether of doctrine, fact, or precept."[2] Many scholars consider Hodge's statements to be nothing

2. Battle, *The Christian Observer.*

more than a weapon used to defend the church against the scientific knowledge which sprang from the era of the Enlightenment.

My inclination would be to reply to this assertion with the same response Bishop Spong replied to the Baptist minister, to wit—"Have you ever read it?"

$\sim$

If the Church is to be honest it must admit to the human origin of the Bible. The Church must explain that in most cases we don't even know who wrote the various books of the Bible, but it is certain that it was written with the worldview of an ancient people, and does not reflect the knowledge or morals of the twenty-first century.

$\sim$

OLD TESTAMENT MIRACLES

Popular Christianity (as understood by the people in the pews)	Academic Christianity (taught in our colleges and seminaries)
There were several miracles performed by "men of God" and by God himself during the time of the Old Testament.	Miracles are the product of creative story tellers. They are used to embellish a hero or a historical event with a theological flavor. Using miracles allows the story teller to make the characters or the events of the story bigger than life, and stir the emotions of the listener.

Theologians have documented fifty-six, so-called miracles in the books of the Old Testament. Some well known, such as Moses and the burning bush and the parting of the Red sea, and some not so well known, such as the thunder that destroyed the Philistines and, perhaps, the sacrifice that was consumed in 1 Kings 18.

Such miracles are usually attributed to the actions of an omnipotent God, a God who intervenes to overrule the laws of nature. But since the Enlightenment period that began in the seventeenth century, many theologians are less likely to proclaim that these are accounts of historical events. There are, of course, many people today who still believe in miracles, but no reputable historian would include in his or her writings, stories of alleged miraculous events. Modern scholars, and modern theologians, regard such reported miracles as either fabrications or cases of mass hallucination.

It is interesting to note that there has never, in recent history, been a miracle acclaimed in an *unambiguous* situation. By that I mean a situation for which there could be no other possible answer but the work of a god. For instance, you will never hear of God restoring the severed limb of an amputee. On the other hand, in every case where a miracle *is* claimed, there are other possible answers—be they ever so remote or coincidental—that could explain the happening.

Miracles were a vital part of the writing style of the ancient world, however, once again, they cannot stand up against reason and scientific knowledge. If one defines a miracle as an act of a god who somehow reaches down and intervenes in the workings of nature in order to favor an individual or group of individuals, then it can be safely said, miracles do not happen, period.

⌒

The church must admit that miracles are, and always have been, events that humans attribute to the hand of God, simply because they have no other way to explain or understand some strange or unusual event. Stories of miracles were a part of the writing style of the ancient world, they were not records of historical events.

⌒

THE SAVIOR MOTIF

Popular Christianity (as understood by the people in the pews)	Academic Christianity (taught in our colleges and seminaries)
The Bible proclaims Jesus (1) was born of a virgin, (2) was the Son of God, (3) performed many miracles, (4) died a cruel death, (5) died to save us from our sins, (6) was resurrected from the grave, (7) was seen by many after raising from the grave, (8) was seen raising into heaven.	The Savior motif is familiar to anyone who studies ancient history. Literally hundreds of men were marked with these words. It was a way of saying, "This was an important person." Such claims are not historical events.

In ancient history we find many so called saviors. Hundreds of kings, warriors and religious icons were given the titles Son of God and Savior. Most of them were said to have been born of a virgin. In addition, they were said to have performed miracles, died a cruel death, died to save humankind from sin, arisen from the grave, been seen by many after arising from the grave, been seen rising into heaven.

Here is but a sample of the Saviors of the ancient world, from the book, *The World's Sixteen Crucified Saviors,* by Hersey Graves;[3] first published in 1875:

> *Tammuz of Mesopotamia 1200 BCE.* Tammuz was a god of Assyria, Babylonia, and Sumeria where he was known as Dumuzi. He is commemorated in the name of the month of June, Du'uzu, the fourth month of a year, which begins at the spring equinox. Tammuz was crucified as an atonement offering: "Trust ye in God, for out of his loins salvation has come unto us." Julius Firmicus speaks of this God rising from the dead for the salvation of the world. This savior which long preceded the advent of Christ, filled the same role in sacred history.
>
> *Wittoba of the Telingonesic 550 BCE.* Wittoba is represented with nail-holes in his hands and the soles of his feet. Nails, hammers and pincers are constantly seen represented on his crucifixes and are objects of adoration among his followers, just as the iron crown of Lombardy has within it a nail claimed to be of "his true original cross," and is much admired and venerated for that reason. The worship of this crucified God prevails

3. Graves, *Saviors,* 120–28.

chiefly in the Travancore and other southern states of India in the region of Madura.

Iao of Nepal 620 BCE. Iao was crucified on a tree in Nepal. The name of this incarnate god and oriental savior occurs frequently in the holy bibles and sacred books of other countries. Some suppose that Iao is the root of the name of the Jewish God, Yehouah (Jehovah), often abbreviated to Yeho.

Hesus of the Celtic Druids 830 BCE. The Celtic Druids depict their god Hesus as having been crucified with a lamb on one side and an elephant on the other, long before the Christian era. The elephant, being the largest animal known, was chosen to represent the magnitude of the sins of the world, while the lamb, from its proverbial innocent nature, was chosen to represent the innocence of the victim, the god offered as a propitiatory sacrifice. The Lamb of God takes away the sins of the world for Christians. The Lamb of God could therefore have been taken from the Druids. This legend was found in Gaul long before Jesus Christ was known to history.

Quezalcoatl of Mexico 580 BCE. Historical authority of the crucifixion of this Mexican god is explicit, unequivocal and ineffaceable. The evidence is tangible, and indelibly engraven upon metal plates. Sometimes he is represented as having been nailed to a cross, sometimes with two thieves hanging with him, and sometimes as hanging with a cross in his hand.

Quirinius of Rome 500 BCE. The crucifixion of this Roman savior is remarkable for the parallel features to that of the Judean savior, not only in the circumstances of his crucifixion, but also in much of his antecedent life. He is represented, like Christ: (1) As having been conceived and brought forth by a virgin. (2) Sought by the reigning king, Amulius, to murder him. (3) As of royal blood, his mother being of kingly descent. (4) As put to death by wicked hands or crucified. (5) At his death, causing the whole earth to have been enveloped in darkness. (6) As being resurrected, and as ascending to heaven.

Prometheus of Caucasus 550 BCE. The crucifixion of Prometheus of Caucasus, described by Seneca, Hesiod, and other writers, states that he was nailed to an upright beam of timber, to which were affixed extended arms of wood, and that this cross was situated near the Caspian Straits. It is doubtful whether there is to be found in the whole range of Greek letters deeper pathos than that of the divine woe of the beneficent demigod Prometheus, crucified on his Scythian crags for his love to mortals. When he died the whole frame of nature became convulsed, the earth shook, the rocks were rent, the graves were opened, and in a storm, which seemed to threaten the dissolution of the universe. The cause for which he suffered was his love for the human race. The whole story of Prometheus's crucifixion, burial and resurrection was acted in pantomime in Athens five hundred years before Christ.

Thulis of Egypt 1700 BCE. This Egyptian savior appears also to have been known as Zulis. After suffering a violent death, he was buried, but rose again, ascended into heaven, and there became the judge of the dead, or of souls in a future state.

He came down from heaven to benefit mankind, and was said to be full of grace and truth.

Indra of Tibet 720 BCE. This Tibetan savior is shown nailed to the cross. There are five wounds, representing the nail-holes and the piercing of the side. Marvelous stories are told of the birth of this Divine Redeemer. His mother was a virgin of black complexion, and hence his complexion was of the ebony hue, as in the case of Christ and some other sin-atoning saviors. He descended from heaven on a mission of benevolence, and ascended back after his crucifixion. He led a life of strict celibacy, which, he taught, was essential to true holiness. He inculcated great tenderness toward all living beings. He could walk upon the water or upon the air and could foretell future events with great accuracy. He practiced the most devout contemplation, severe discipline of the body and mind, and completely subdued his passions. He was worshipped as a god who had existed as a spirit from all eternity, and his followers were called Heavenly Teachers.

Alcestos of Euripides 600 BCE. A less usual crucified God was Alcestos, who was female, the only example of a feminine God atoning for the sins of the world upon the cross. The doctrine of the trinity and atoning offering for sin was inculcated as a part of her religion.

Crite of Chaldaea 1200 BCE. The Chaldeans have noted in their sacred books the crucifixion of this god. He was also known as the Redeemer, and was styled the Ever Blessed Son of God, the savior of the Race, the Atoning Offering for an Angry God. When he was offered up, both heaven and earth were shaken to their foundations.

Mithras of Persia 600 BCE. This Persian God was slain upon the cross to make atonement for mankind, and to take away the sins of the world. He was born on the twenty-fifth day of December, and crucified on a tree. Christian writers both speak of his being slain, and yet both omit to speak of the manner in which he was put to death.

Were there literally hundreds of virgin births? Of course not. Were there literally hundreds of saviors? Of course not. Scholars, both secular and Christian, explain that these things were written about men of honor, men of high esteem, to say; "This was a special person, in this person we have seen the divine, remember him."

The Savior Motif is so common and so repeatable that even the proclaimed miracles in many cases are the same from one Savior to the next—changing water into wine, raising the dead, healing the lepers, walking on water, to name a few. The Savior Motif was commonplace in the ancient world.

Christianity has continually downplayed or overlooked this part of history and, in fact, there are many stories of Christian censorship and obliteration of scrolls, tablets and codices in order to suppress the memory of such historical events (other that those of Jesus of Nazareth).

Modern scholarship explains Jesus in two phases; the historical Jesus who lived and died prior to the Easter story, and the post-Easter Jesus that was a creation of the church, after his death. It is this post-Easter Jesus story that contains the Savior Motif. The same is true for all the other so called saviors. Their stories were written/created years after their death.

This knowledge (that Jesus was not literally born of a virgin, that he was not literally the Son of God, nor did he die to save us from our sins), has dramatic consequences for the Christian faith.

～

If the church has any intention of becoming intellectually honest with its constituency, it must put aside its ancient (and now immature) beliefs in the "Savior Motif" and explain these historical writings for what they were and are. Simply expressions of love and admiration for a person of history.

～

NEW TESTAMENTS MIRACLES

Popular Christianity (as understood by the people in the pews)	Academic Christianity (taught in our colleges and seminaries)
Jesus performed many miracles during his years of ministry to the people. These are testaments to his divinity.	The miracles of the New Testament are in every respect the same as those of the Old Testament. They are written to extol the virtue of the one about whom they are written. Miracles, if defined as an act or event caused by a supernatural being interceding in the laws of nature, do not exist.

Many of the New Testament miracles can be explained as part of the Savior Motif. They appear again and again in other stories of Saviors written hundreds of years before the life of Jesus. Stories of so called Saviors walking on water, raising the dead, healing the lepers, changing water to wine, can be found throughout ancient history.

Other of the New Testament miracles are replications or expansions of Old Testament miracles. They are intended to show that Jesus is the new Moses, the new Elijah, the new Elisha. They are an attempt to say that the God of the Old Testament is found in the Jesus of Christianity. Most scholars today doubt that these miracle stories were interpreted as reports of historical events even at the time they were written. It is only with the passage of time and the emphasis placed upon them by our literal reading of the Bible that has distorted their meaning such that some today think of them as literal events. In his book, *Jesus for the Non-Religious,* Bishop John Shelby Spong does a wonderful job of explaining the linkage between the miracles of the Old and New Testaments. I highly recommend it for your reading.

$\sim$

The church must educate the people in the pews on the subject of miracles. There is no parent figure in the sky reaching down from time to time to alter the laws of nature to cause a river to stop flowing, or to cause a blind man to see. There has never in the history of the world been a miracle healing of a case of cancer. There has never been a football game won by a miracle field goal. There has never ever been a person saved from death in an automobile accident because God miraculously

*reached down and protected him or her . . . never. The church
knows this to be true and must end its silence on the subject.*

~

THE ATONEMENT

Popular Christianity (as understood by the people in the pews)	Professional Christianity (taught in our colleges and seminaries)
Jesus was sent—by God—from heaven to earth, to suffer and die as an atonement for the sins of all mankind. This was the central purpose of the life and death of Jesus.	The first mention of the idea of Jesus dying for the sins of mankind appears in the writings of Paul (Gal 1:4, Rom 5:6–8, 1 Cor 8:11, 2 Cor 5:14–15, 1 Thes 5:10). The concept of atonement was later expounded upon by St. *Augustine* of Hippo, a fifth-century theologian. It is a manmade concept.

In the Old Testament the Day of Atonement was an annual day of repentance for the people of Israel. A day to ask God for the forgiveness of their sins. The ritual of Atonement is prescribed in the Old Testament book of Leviticus chapter 16 (also Lev 23:27–31, Lev 25:9, Exod 30:10, Num 29:7–11). It is described as a solemn fast, during which no food or drink could be consumed, and all work was forbidden.

During the ritual, the high priest was to offer an animal sacrifice upon the alter, as an atonement—forgiveness of sins—for himself and for the people. The Bible calls this, *Yom Hakippurim* (Hebrew for Day of Atonement), which the Jewish religion celebrates today as *Yom Kippur.*

Now let us look at another Jewish holiday, called Pasach (Hebrew) or Passover (English), which celebrates and remembers the freeing of the Hebrews from slavery in ancient Egypt. The origin of the story appears in the twelfth chapter of Exodus. The Hebrews had been held as slaves in Egypt for many years. God allegedly chose Moses to lead them out of bondage. When Moses repeatedly asked the Pharaoh of Egypt to let the people of Israel leave his land, the Pharaoh repeatedly refused. As a result, God caused a series of plagues to come upon Egypt.

In the tenth and final plague, God caused an angel of death to pass over the entire land of Egypt and kill the firstborn offspring of every household, both humans and animals. To provide protection from the angel of death for the children of Israel, God instructed the Hebrew people to sprinkle the blood of a sacrificed lamb on the two side doorposts of the house and on the upper doorpost, called a lintel. The angel, upon seeing the blood, would "pass over" that house and not destroy its firstborn. Hence the sacrificial lamb was called the "Passover" lamb. In carrying out this commandment from God to use the slain lamb, the Hebrew people protected themselves from the angel of death.

This alleged slaughter of the firstborn of the Egyptians seemed to convince the Pharaoh that God was serious and he subsequently let the Hebrews go!

Later, as Moses was leading the Hebrews through the wilderness of the Sinai, God commanded that they should— according to Numbers 9:3—celebrate and remember the event of the "pass over" annually. Thus the celebration called Pasach or Passover came into being and is still celebrated today among the Jewish communities of the world.

Now, fast forward from the Old Testament to the year 56 CE, to the day Paul's letter to the church at Corinth was received by that little group of followers. We call the letter 1 Corinthians. We don't actually know how little or big the group at Corinth was. It could have been six people, or it could have been sixty or even six hundred. We just don't know.

On that day, the people gathered either in the synagogue, or perhaps someone's home, or maybe in some public place to have one of their number read this letter, just received, from this self-proclaimed itinerant preacher/apostle named Paul.

I have stood in the ruins of those homes in Corinth. I have walked up the steps of the synagogue there. I stood in the public meeting place and listened to the letter from Paul to the Corinthians being read . . . but that was in 2005.

In 56 CE the church at Corinth was having problems. Apparently discipline problems among its members were rampant. Paul was writing in an attempt to get them to straighten up, get their act together, so to speak.

I'll not read the entire letter, just one sentence from chapter 5 where he writes,[4]

> "For our Passover feast is ready, now that Christ, our Passover lamb, has been sacrificed."

Paul was likening Jesus to the Passover lamb that the Hebrews sacrificed each year in remembrance of their

4. 1 Cor 5:7, *Today's English Version.*

protection from the angel of death. But as we discover by reading further, Paul was calling Jesus the sacrificial lamb that released us, all humankind, from the bondage of both sin and death. He seems to be combining the meaning of two separate events in Hebrew history, into one—Atonement, the forgiveness of sin and Passover, release from the power of death.

Had I been there that day in 56 CE, I think I would have spoken up at that point and said to the reader, "Wait, wait… read that part again, please."

> *"For our Passover feast is ready, now that Christ,*
> *our Passover lamb, has been sacrificed."*

I may have stood and listened in silence to the rest of the letter, but then I think I would have hurried to my home and searched for a piece of parchment, and I would have penned a letter to be carried back to Paul—he had written from Ephesus.

I would have written something like this:

Dear Sir,

We just finished the reading of your letter. Thank you for your concern for the people of Corinth. It is very kind of you. However, I have one question. By what authority have you called this man Jesus, "our Passover lamb"? Where did you come by the idea that he was sacrificed for us?

This is a very important question, because, on Paul's simple statement hinges the entire church doctrine of Atonement and Salvation. Paul made a giant leap to proclaim Jesus to be the Passover lamb, with the unexplained twist that, whereas the Passover lamb had triggered the Hebrew's protection from the angel of death and freedom from the Egyptians, Jesus as Passover lamb had freed all humans, for all time, from both sin and death. Paul said it, the people accepted it—apparently without question—and for the ensuing two thousand years, it has dominated the doctrine of the Christian church. It has been called the centerpiece of the Christian faith.

But I ask you, by what authority . . . what special knowledge . . . what evidence did Paul make such a self serving, egocentric proclamation?

The answers, of course, are . . . none . . . none . . . and none! No authority, no special knowledge, and no evidence.

Where could Paul have gotten such a story? Did he make it up? Did he have a dream? Did this thought come to him through meditation or prayer? Did he base it on his interpretation of some portion of ancient scripture? Was it a part of the oral tradition of the day? We are not given any indication of any of these possibilities. Yet the church has followed this vague line of self-delusional thinking ever since.

I wish I could have had the opportunity to query Paul about that statement and the similar statements he made to the Galatians, the Thessalonians, the Romans, the Ephesians, and others.

Perhaps Paul, knowing that many nations and many other religions of that era had deemed certain of their heroes "Savior," thought it would be quite all right for him to promote Jesus to the same status. It was not an uncommon practice. If he could convince people to believe such a thing it would certainly strengthen his cause as well.

Paul wrote nothing of the teachings of Jesus, only that he died for the salvation of all humankind. Something that was totally foreign to anything Jesus had ever said or taught.

So, by what authority did he declare these things to be true? By what special knowledge? By what evidence?

Unfortunately the answers still seem to be . . . none . . . none . . .and none!

Some scholars accuse Paul of kidnapping the church with his idea of atonement/salvation. The idea is diametrically opposed to the teachings of Jesus. Jesus taught us to care for others. He taught us to help the poor, to reach out to the downtrodden and those at the fringe of society. Paul on the other hand taught an egocentric message of self preservation. In all of the thirteen books of the New Testament attributed to Paul, there is not a word about the teachings of Jesus.

The leaders of the new Christian movement, in Jerusalem, James and Peter, espoused a doctrine like that of Jesus. Once the Jesus movement split from the Jewish religion for good in 88 CE, however, the Pauline version became dominate and has remained so ever since.

~

The church must come to grips with the myth of atonement. It must begin to speak honestly with the people in the pews about this ancient belief—where it came from and why it was so appealing to the Gentile world. The church must assure its adherents that each human is responsible for his or her own behavior. No one has died to redeem another for their actions. Atonement, like so many of the church's doctrines, is a purely human construct.

~

THE TRINITY

Popular Christianity (as understood by the people in the pews)	Academic Christianity (taught in our colleges and seminaries)
Christian doctrine holds that God is one, but that three distinct "persons" constitute the one God: the Father, the Son, and the Holy Spirit. This threefold God of Christian belief is referred to as the Trinity.	The word Trinity is found in neither the Old nor the New Testament. The idea of the Trinity did not appear until the fourth century CE. It is a human concept and has no basis in reality.

What follows is an excerpt from the text of a sermon I gave some years ago, on the subject of the Trinity. I use it here to help you, the reader, understand the history of the Trinity.

$\sim$

Perhaps the most interesting, most absorbing, and at the same time, the most confusing item of Christian doctrine, something that you and I are exposed to in almost every worship service, is called the Holy Trinity. Many church leaders state that the Trinity is the term employed to signify the central doctrine of the Christian religion. Nearly all Christian churches agree that the Trinity is the fundamental doctrine of Christianity.

The confusion for me, and I suspect for you as well, comes in our attempt to conceptualize the idea of this very important doctrine, which, when simply stated says: God is triune, that is, the Father is totally God, the Son is totally

God, the Holy Spirit is totally God. And yet, there are not three Gods but only one. Each is said to be without beginning, having existed for eternity. Each is said to be almighty, with each neither greater nor lesser than the other, and yet they are only one.

You and I, the people in the pews, sing of this Holy Trinity in the Doxology: Praise God from whom all blessings flow, / Praise him all creatures here below, / Praise him above ye heavenly hosts, / Praise Father, Son and Holy Ghost.

As a youth, I often thought that referring to the Holy Spirit as *the Holy Ghost* was border-line blasphemy but I guess not, it's in our hymn books and other religious documents. Yet I always felt uncomfortable about the phrase *Holy Ghost*—not nearly as uncomfortable, however, as when some of my friends in our youth group would refer to the Trinity as, "Daddy-o, JC, and the spook!" But that's another story.

The Encyclopedia Americana notes that the doctrine of the Trinity is considered to be beyond the grasp of human reason.

Joseph Bracken mirrors that confusion in his book, *What Are They Saying About the Trinity?*[5]

> Christian professionals who with considerable effort learned about the Trinity during their seminary years hesitate to present it to their people from the pulpit, even on Trinity Sunday. Why should they bore people with something that in the end they wouldn't properly understand anyway?

5. Bracken, *What Are They Saying*, 3.

Perhaps then, with all of this, you and I, the people in the pews, need not feel badly if we are somewhat confused by this rather unwieldy doctrine.

But inquiring minds want to know, and I—for good or ill—have one of those inquiring minds.

One of my first questions regarding this doctrine had to be, "How did such a confusing doctrine originate?" Little did I know where that question would lead me.

My first inclination was to turn to the Bible. Surely the Bible should clearly reveal information about a matter as fundamental as the Trinity is claimed to be. But I was amazed to discover that the word Trinity is not to be found in the Bible.

Okay, while the word Trinity is not found in the Bible, perhaps at least the *idea* of the Trinity is there. For instance, what do the Hebrew Scriptures—the Old Testament—reveal?

Well, the Encyclopedia of Religion states: "Theologians today are in agreement that the Hebrew Bible does not contain a doctrine of the Trinity." [6] And the New Catholic Encyclopedia also states: "The doctrine of the Holy Trinity is not taught in the Old Testament." [7]

Edmund Fortman, in his book, *The Triune God,* writes this: "The Old Testament writings about God neither express nor imply any idea of, or belief in, a plurality or trinity of persons within the one Godhead" [8]

An examination of the Old Testament shows this to be true. There is no clear teaching of a Trinity in the first

6. LaCugna "*Trinity,*" Vol. 14, 9360.

7. Draina, "*Holy Trinity,*" Vol. 14, 201.

8. Fortman, *The Triune God,* 9.

thirty-nine books of the Bible that make up the canon of the Hebrew Scriptures.

Well then, what about the Christian Scriptures, or New Testament as they are also known? Do they speak of a Trinity?

The Encyclopedia Britannica states: "Neither the word Trinity nor the explicit doctrine appear in the New Testament."[9] In his book, *A Short History of Christian Doctrine,* author Bernhard Lohse says: "As far as the New Testament is concerned, one does not find in it, an actual doctrine of the Trinity." [10]

So, I discovered, neither the thirty-nine books of the Hebrew Scriptures nor the twenty-seven books of the Christian Scriptures provide any teaching of the Trinity.

To say the least, I was surprised. But if the Trinity is not a Biblical teaching, how did it become a Christian doctrine?

Well, I learned some people believe that it happened at the Council of Nicaea, in Greece, in the year 325 CE. But that is not totally correct. The Council of Nicaea did state that Jesus was made "of the same substance" as God, but it did not establish the Trinity. There was not even the mention of the Holy Spirit as the third person of a triune Godhead at Nicaea.

The Roman Emperor Constantine had called the Council of Nicaea. Constantine was aware there was a debate in the church over the issue of the divinity of Jesus, and he surmised that such a religious division was a threat to his empire. So he called the bishops together to settle the issue once and for all. But after two months of debate and

9. Unknown, "*Trinity,*" Vol. 11, 928.

10. Lohse, *A Short History,* 38.

no resolution in sight, this pagan politician, emperor, and warrior intervened and decided the issue in favor of those who said that Jesus was "of one substance with the Father." Constantine had basically no understanding whatsoever of the question, but he knew he wanted to solidify his domain.

But remember, none of the debate at Nicaea was over the issue of a Trinity.

After Nicaea, the debate about Jesus continued for decades. Those who believed that Jesus was not equal to God actually came back into favor for a period of time. Then in 381 CE, Emperor Theodosius convened yet another Church Council, this one in Constantinople, to clarify the formula again.

It was at this Council, in 381 CE, that the bishops decided to place the Holy Spirit on the same level as God. And so for the first time, Christianity's Trinity began to come into focus. It did not appear as part of a creed, however, until somewhere in the late fifth or early sixth century when the Athanasian creed is first reported to have been used.

So that the reader might appreciate the convoluted style of this creed, I print a portion of it here:

> Whosoever will be saved, before all things it is necessary that he hold the catholic faith. Which faith except every one do keep whole and undefiled, without doubt he shall perish everlastingly. And the catholic faith is this: that we worship one God in Trinity, and Trinity in unity. Neither confounding the persons, nor dividing the substance. For there is one person of the Father, another of the Son, and another of the Holy Spirit. But the Godhead of the Father, of the Son, and

of the Holy Spirit is all one, the glory equal, the majesty coeternal. Such as the Father is, such is the Son, and such is the Holy Spirit. The Father uncreated, the Son uncreated, and the Holy Spirit uncreated. The Father incomprehensible, the Son incomprehensible, and the Holy Spirit incomprehensible. The Father eternal, the Son eternal and the Holy Spirit eternal. And yet there are not three eternals but one eternal. As also there are not three uncreated nor three incomprehensible, but one uncreated and one incomprehensible.

So likewise, the Father is almighty, the Son almighty, and the Holy Spirit almighty. And yet they are not three almighties but one almighty. So the Father is God, the Son is God, and the Holy Spirit is God. And yet there are not three Gods, but one God. So likewise the Father is Lord, the Son is Lord, and the Holy Spirit is Lord. And yet there are not three Lords but one Lord. For like as we are compelled by the Christian verity to acknowledge every Person by himself to be God and Lord; so we are forbidden by the catholic religion to say; there are three Gods or three Lords. The Father is made of none, neither created nor begotten. The Son is of the Father alone; not made nor created, but begotten. The Holy Spirit is of the father and of the Son; neither made, nor created, nor begotten, but proceeding.

So there is one Father, not three Fathers; one Son, not three Sons; one Holy Spirit, not three holy spirits. And in this Trinity, none is afore or after another; none is greater or less than another. But the whole three Persons are coeternal, and coequal. So that in all things, as aforesaid, the Unity in Trinity and the Trinity in Unity is to be worshiped. He, therefore, that will be saved, must thus think of the Trinity . . . (and on and on . . .)

My search for the origins of the doctrine of the Trinity had come to an end!

But now two more, perhaps more important questions, came to mind: Who were these men that made this momentous proclamation? And, by what authority did they make it?

To answer the first question—Who were these men?—we must try to travel back to the fourth century. The worldview of that era was quite different than the worldview of today. People of that era believed the earth was flat, that it rested on a bed of water, and the blue sky above was a canopy; beyond which was heaven and the almighty God. And this blue canopy was just a few hundred feet above us.

To be literate in the fourth century meant you could spell your name. That might be a slight exaggeration, but certainly no more than 4 or 5 percent of the population were literate.

Few churches possessed a Bible. Most religious understanding was passed from person to person through oral tradition. This accounts for the many diverse beliefs within Christianity in that era. The thought occurs to me that in that regard, things haven't changed that much, have they?

The bishops of the church were, of course, men who held this same worldview. Perhaps educated by the standards of that time and place but certainly not intellectually astute by today's standards.

As to the question of authority, well they certainly had the authority to decide for the church what the church would believe as doctrine, (after all they were the bishops) but as far as their ability to decide that such a thing was true, factual, or physically correct, they had absolutely no such knowledge whatsoever. They performed no investigation, no experiments, no DNA tests. They simply debated the issue, took a vote and proclaimed it to be true. There was absolutely nothing to substantiate such a claim.

These unnamed, unknown men who were, by today's standards semi-literate at best, simply decreed that it was so, and for the ensuing 1500 years we Christians have believed as literal truth, that the Father the Son and the Holy Spirit are all of the same substance, not three but one, not one but three, etc., etc. *ad nauseam.*

There are many stories like the one about the Trinity. The Church history is replete with legends and symbols, that you and I, the people in the pews, have been taught to believe as literal truth. Yet the real message of the Trinity lies not in the Trinity itself, but behind the Trinity, in the reason why those ancient bishops felt compelled to relate such a story.

~

The church must, once again, explain to the people in the pews that the foundation of the doctrine of the Trinity is nothing more than human thought. It was made up to add prestige and stature to the Godhead of the church and has no validity beyond its human source.

~

ORIGINAL SIN

Popular Christianity (as understood by the people in the pews)	Professional Christianity (taught in our colleges and seminaries)
Adam and Eve committed the "original sin" when they disobeyed God and ate the forbidden fruit in the Garden of Eden. This sin is transmitted from parent to child through every generation.	The idea of "original sin" is a human concept, having no basis in reality.

Original sin is said to result from the Fall of Man, when Adam and Eve ate the forbidden fruit of a particular tree in the Garden of Eden. This first sin, an action of the first human beings, is traditionally understood to be the cause of "original sin," the fallen state from which human beings can be saved only by God's grace.

The reader may be shocked to learn that the doctrine of original sin is not found in the Bible. It was first developed in the second century by a man named Saint Irenaeus, the Bishop of Lyon in southern France. Irenaeus was born around 125 CE and died about 202 CE. It—the concept of original sin—was further developed by St. Augustine of Hippo (354 to 430), of Algeria, North Africa. Augustine is one of the most important figures in the development of the concept of original sin. He taught that original sin was physically transmitted from parent to child through the concupiscence—roughly, lust—that accompanied sexual reproduction, weakening the human will and making humanity a "condemned crowd."

In Augustine's view—which is called Realism—all of humanity was really present in Adam when he sinned, and therefore all humans are sinners. Original sin, according to Augustine, consists of the guilt of Adam which all human beings inherit. Therefore, as sinners, we human beings are utterly depraved in nature, lacking the freedom to do good, and cannot respond to the will of God without divine grace.

St. Augustine believed that the only possible destinations for the human soul are heaven and hell. He believed that infants, who die before being baptized, go to hell as a consequence of original sin. The church fathers who followed Augustine adopted his position, which became a point of reference for Latin theologians in the Middle Ages.

St. Augustine's idea of original sin was popular among Protestant reformers, such as Martin Luther and John Calvin, and also within Roman Catholic Church. But like other traditional church doctrines, original sin has been denied or reinterpreted by various modern Christian denominations and theologians.

What we have here is: an imaginary god, an imaginary creation story, a "perfect" man and woman, and a talking snake, all coming together in an imaginary garden. Then thousands of years later some zelous religious leaders concluding that the actions of the rebellious, imaginary man and woman have somehow been passed down from generation to generation to every man, woman, and child that has ever been or ever will be born.

~

The church must explain to its adherents that Original Sin is nothing more than a human idea, a doctrine invented by those who were promoting the Christian religion. Its original intent, in my opinion, might well have been to induce fear in the masses and cause them to flock to the church to seek redemtion.

~

THE SECOND COMING OF JESUS

Popular Christianity (as understood by the people in the pews)	Academic Christianity (taught in our colleges and seminaries)
Many Christians believe that Jesus ascended into heaven at the completion of his mortal ministry, and two angels declared to his apostles, "This same Jesus, which is taken up from you into heaven, shall so come in like manner as ye have seen him go into heaven." (Acts 1:11). Since that time, believers have looked forward to the second coming of Jesus Christ.	This idea of the Second Coming of Jesus —known in theological circles as the Parousia—is a human-made concept. It is part of the messianic prophecy, which declares Jesus to be the Son of God. It was developed in the post-Easter era of the developing Church. It has no basis in reality.

The idea of Jesus' return to Earth or what most Christians call "the Second Coming" is mentioned several times in the New Testament of the Bible—although it is not called the Second Coming. Christian doctrine stresses again and again that followers of "the Way" should be ever vigilant and prepared for his arrival. The New Testament also describes how his coming may happen at any time, even when we least expect it. Even today, many Christians anticipate the imminent arrival of Christ and look forward to his second coming.

In the first few centuries of the early Christian church, there were many who lived in a state of expectation that the end may soon be upon them.

Christians living in the first few decades after Jesus died believed that he would return to earth at any moment. But as time went on and he did not appear, the idea of the second coming began to fade. Although there were many predictions of his return—which of course did not come true—followers began to become skeptical.

In the late fourth century St. Augustine—whom I mentioned earlier wrote about the idea of Original Sin— began to promote the acceptance of such things as the Second Coming and the end times as symbolic or figurative rather than predictions of actual future events. These ideas became quite popular until after the Christian Reformation in the sixteenth century. Prior to this time the reading and interpretation of the Bible was primarily the domain of the church officials, but now, with the aid of the Gutenberg printing press, the ordinary layman could read the scriptures and form his or her own interpretation. Many chose once again to believe that the scriptures were a foretelling of actual future events.

In the nineteenth century an Englishman named John Nelson Darby (1800–1882) invented his own twist on the idea of the Second Coming. In his version, Jesus would appear in the sky and take all the good Christians who had been baptized to a safe place. This is where we get the term "The Rapture." Then Jesus would supposedly destroy and rebuild the earth and return the Christians to a happy and prosperous life. Many Christian denominations—primarily Evangelicals and Pentecostals—still preach and teach Darby's invented prophecies of the second coming of Jesus

In all of this, one must keep in mind that the whole idea of the second coming of Jesus is inextricably linked to the human concept of God as a supernatural being. Once the supernatural God idea is understood for what it is, the Second Coming becomes nonsensical.

～

The Church must admit to the people in the pews that the idea of the Second Coming is ancient folklore and has not been taught, in reputable seminaries, as a valid concept, for decades.

～

LIFE AFTER DEATH

Popular Christianity (as understood by the people in the pews)	Academic Christianity (taught in our colleges and seminaries)
If you believe that Jesus is the Son of the living God and repent of your sins, when you die, you will live in heaven for eternity. Those who do not believe and do not repent will spend eternity in hell.	The concept of a life after death based on a reward/ punishment philosophy existed prior to the forming of Christianity. It is a behavior-control tool used to control the masses and provide hope in the face of finite mortality. There is no literal heaven or hell to which humans ascend or descend after death.

Although, the idea of an afterlife can be seen in the earliest of religions, evidence from archeological excavations suggest that humans believed in some kind of life after death long before we began to form religious notions.[11]

The earliest recorded concepts regarding death and afterlife come from Persia, Egypt, and later Greece. It is thought that the early beliefs of the ancient Israelites about life after death were derived from Middle Eastern pagan cultures. Later Jewish beliefs concerning heaven and hell may have incorporated ideas from the Zoroastrian religion of Persia and the Greek pagan culture.

According to historian and sociologist Harry E. Barnes, the earliest ideas of afterlife probably began with

11. Allen, *The Evolution*, 23–32.

the concept known as animism.[12] This idea is basically defined as the belief in immortality of one's spiritual self continuing to exist after life. Barnes suggests the creation of the supernatural being and the idea of an afterlife were actually originated by man himself as opposed to an almighty being that created life. In other words, the idea of entering into another life after death came about from the ideas and needs of man.

Perhaps Sigmund Freud put it most succinctly when he said that belief in the afterlife can be safely dismissed because it is simply a case of wish fulfillment.[13] He basically said that humans have a juvenile desire to survive death, so we made up the idea of an afterlife.

⌢

As difficult as it will be for Christians—or people of any religion for that matter—to hear the truth, the church must admit that there is simply no rational reason to believe that any form of life or existence continues after the demise of our earthly body.

⌢

Obviously, once these ten doctrines are redefined it will be necessary to re-evaluate and redefine several others as well. Such items as prayer, worship, the Eucharist, and other sacraments make little or no sense when viewed with this new understanding of God and religion. However, that does not mean they cannot take on new meaning and value.

The church has postponed the task of redefining and re-evaluating its doctrine for too many years and is now

12. Barnes, *An Intellectual*, 3rd rev. ed. Vol. 1, 46.
13. Freud, *The Future of an Illusion*, 38–42.

paying the consequences of declining attendance and membership. Continuing to deny that these changes are needed will simply exacerbate the situation and lead to further losses.

4

Take a Deep Breath . . .

I<small>F YOU</small> have stayed with me this far, you are perhaps feeling a good bit of stress or frustration—maybe even anger and disbelief. You may be learning about things that seem foreign to everything you have ever been taught about your religion—things that tear away at the very core of your belief system. So, sit back for a moment and take a deep breath . . . Let me remind you why I am writing this book. My purpose is to:

- help shake the Church—or rather the Church officials—into understanding the severity of the current situation, hoping something positive might begin to happen to bring more intellectual honesty to the Christian faith,

- once again make the Christian faith a relevant part of the intellectual world of the twenty-first century,

- make the Christian faith something that will appeal to educated and uneducated alike,

- make Christianity a religion that does not ask its adherents to believe folklore and myth as fact, and

- make Christianity a religion that does not ask its

adherents to leave their brains at home when they come to church on Sunday morning.

Please believe me when I say, I am not out to destroy the church, to the contrary, my purpose is, in the end, to help save it. If my method seems harsh, may I remind you that I told you in the beginning I would not "candy coat" my comments. There has been, in my opinion, too much of that approach in the past.

The doctrines of Popular Christianity I have been talking about must be understood for what they are—myth and folklore. Not that that is a bad thing, just that Christianity must come to grips with the fact that the writers of the Bible lived in a society with a different worldview, which included a much different understanding of the universe, nature, and the human condition than we have today. We must no longer tolerate being taught that such things are factual and historical truth. Our church leaders have had their heads (and ours) "stuck in the sand" for much to long. Pretending that everything is all right, is killing the church.

Myth and folklore, when explained as such, can add greatly to the religious experience. But when spoken of as factual or historical truth, it can breed distrust and contempt among the more educated of today's society. Still, pastors in most (but not all) Christian churches continue to preach without making a distinction between fact and myth.

I recently attended a worship service in which the pastor was relating the story of Jesus walking on water.[1] He spoke of the story as if it were an actual historical event. His words gave every indication that Jesus and Peter had indeed

1. Matt 14:22–23.

violated the laws of nature, Jesus, by his divine powers and Peter, by his faith in Jesus. His message was one of trust in the teachings of Jesus. I ask myself, "Would the message have been any less vivid had the pastor indicated that the 'walking on water' story was not necessarily a true story?" My personal belief is that it would have been a *stronger* message had he done so. Why? Because it would have been honest. And once the story was exposed as myth the question could have been asked, "What was there about this man Jesus that caused people to tell such stories about him?"

Increasing our understanding of ancient mythology can do nothing but strengthen our appreciation for the stories of the Bible. This is true especially when we strip away the need to believe in supernaturalism and superstition. Such beliefs were common place in the ancient world— even as recent as the sixteenth century—but it is counter productive to expect educated people to believe such tales as factual. Spittle and dirt placed on a blind man's eyes will not give him back his sight. God does not, and never has, stopped the sun in its travel across the sky. No god of any kind has ever stepped out onto a cloud and spoken to a gathering of people below. Such writings were accepted in the unscientific world of the past, but they are nonsensical today unless honestly explained.

Many in the church believe that the Bible will lose its power if exposed to questioning and critical examination. I contend just the opposite is true. I believe the Bible is loosing its power because the church is refusing to press forward with the knowledge already recognized by the clergy and Christian scholars. An honest and mature belief will emerge to replace the child-like belief of the past, and Christianity will benefit greatly.

The church must not continue to ask people to believe myth and folklore as factual history. The laity must be treated as the adults they are, not the children the church would like them to be. They deserve to be treated as competent people, able to face the world as well as any in the academic ranks. Maintaining the secrecy about the true nature of the Bible will only perpetuate the downward spiral that has persisted for some six decades.

5

Questioning Our Imagination

I DO not claim to be any sort of expert on the subject of the human brain. I have, however, read enough on this topic to feel comfortable in offering some thoughts for the reader to consider, as it relates to our personal belief systems. Nothing I say here should be taken as definitive, rather, I should hope it should prompt the reader to do further investigation. A great deal of information has been gathered in the past decade about how the human brain functions and how we as individuals are affected by various stimuli in our genetics and our environment.

The questions we could ask, with regard to the subject matter of this book, might be, "Why does our brain allow us to believe things for which there is no evidence whatsoever?" "How can an adult mind validate ideas, concepts, or stories of the supernatural that others find to be irrational, even nonsensical?"

Of course, there is no simple definitive answer to such questions, but certainly it can't be that we simply believe such things out of shear ignorance. If that were the case, education alone would almost always be the answer, but it is not. Many who believe in the supernatural, for instance, are well-educated people. Many of them will explain that they have experienced the presence of the supernatural or have seen the supernatural at work in someone's life. There is no doubt in their mind that the supernatural exists, and for them the supernatural means God. No amount of education or explanation will change their mind.

You might explain to them, that in every case where they felt or witnessed the presence of the supernatural, there could have been several other explanations, but you would be wasting your time. You could explain that chance and coincidence play a much bigger role in such matters than most people realize, but your words would not be convincing.

So what is it that causes some (perhaps most) humans to believe the irrational and/or illogical? Do the people who study such phenomena have an answer?

In the past decade, tremendous advances have been made in the field of cognitive neuroscience. Much has been written about the development of the human brain and our thought processes. Even so, there is still much that scientists do not know and may never know about why we believe what we believe.

Let me explain, as best I can, some of the theory that has been advanced regarding the tendencies of humans to harbor beliefs in the supernatural.

One such theory suggests that many of the beliefs an individual holds, come from what we were taught as infants and toddlers. It could very well be that our survival as a species has been dependent upon the fact that as infants and toddlers we are very gullible. It may be that an evolutionary propensity toward listening and learning at a very young age gave us an edge that allowed us to live and pass those traits on to our offspring. When the early cave-mother told her children, "Don't go too close to the edge of the cliff," or "Stay away from that saber tooth tiger," she knew what she was talking about! And those of her brood who learned the lessons quickly and succinctly lived to play another day and eventually produce offspring of their own.

We know that most children are trusting of what their parents tell them, thus when today's mother tells her children, "Don't play in the street," or "If you pray to God, he will protect you," such messages are imprinted in their young minds. And when the message contains supernatural characters like God, the Devil, angels, Santa, Easter Bunny, or the Tooth Fairy, they are all the more easy to remember.

Another theory has to do with our inability to understand complex scientific explanations. The average person does not have a degree in science. Therefore, we often do not comprehend scientific language. We get confused or perhaps interpret information wrongly. Perhaps we hear the words "scientific theory" and take that to mean, an educated "guess" when in fact a scientific theory is an idea that has been proven beyond a reasonable doubt.

At the same time, however, we feel a need to have answers to life's important questions, and since the supernatural stories seem plausible to our unscientific mind, we stick with them until such time as we may become educated to a more scientific understanding.

There is another category of individual that we might call, "The uninformed, who choose to remain uninformed." My experience tells me there are millions of people who fit well into this category with regard to religious beliefs. They are the ones who would be comfortable with the bumper sticker that reads, "God said it, I believe it, that settles it." Let me relate a conversation I recently had that exemplified this point.

I was speaking with a gentleman I will call Sam (not his real name). Somewhere in the conversation I mentioned something about religious objects found in Europe, which archeologists say are at least forty thousand years old.

Sam's response was, "How do they know they are that old? I don't believe they can tell."

"Sure they can," I replied, "Carbon dating can tell us the age of objects within just a very few years."

Sam smiled and said, "That's what they say, but I don't believe it."

"Why don't you believe it?" I asked.

"They could tell you anything. You don't know," said Sam.

"But," I contested, "carbon dating is a proven science. It has been used for dating objects for decades. It's not something new or mysterious."

Sam shook his head, "Well, I don't believe it."

"Have you ever read anything about carbon dating, how it is done?"

"Nope," was Sam's repy.

"Do you know what the principle of radioactive carbon fourteen isotope decay is all about?" I asked.

"Nope."

"Then why are you so sure it doesn't work? You know nothing about it, you've read nothing about it. How can you say you don't believe it works?"

"Well, I don't. I think they just make that stuff up to prove whatever point they want to make."

I decided not to pursue the conversation any further. Nothing I could say was going to change Sam's mind, and I doubt very much he will ever make the effort to educate himself on the subject of carbon dating. He will probably go to his grave disbelieving a very sound scientific principle. Sam is content with forming his opinion on the validity of carbon dating from an uninformed and uneducated bias.

Does it matter? In the totality of things does it really matter what Sam believes or doesn't believe about carbon dating? Well, perhaps not, as it relates to Sam alone. But consider the influence Sam may have on the beliefs of his children and grandchildren. Now we are talking about possibly perpetuating Sam's lack of belief in scientific information on to future generations.

If we extrapolate Sam's reluctance toward becoming educated on a given subject, like carbon dating, to the realm of belief in the supernatural, perhaps the reader will see what I mean by, "The uninformed, who choose to remain uninformed."

Many "believers" will not allow themselves to ask questions or study any material that might disrupt their "uninformed" beliefs in the supernatural. Thus, the religious maturity of a great portion of the human species is prevented from evolving to a higher level.

I do not agree with the contention that we humans need to believe in imaginary gods in order to calm our fear of mortality. Perhaps it was the case in the past but in this age, I find it to be little more than naive ignorance. Perhaps my position is better stated in a quote from the twentieth-century British philosopher and social critic, Bertrand Russell.

There is something feeble and a little contempt-
ible about a man who cannot face the perils
of life without the help of comfortable myths.
Almost inevitably some part of him is aware that
they are myths and that he believes them only
because they are comforting. But he dare not
face this thought! Moreover, since he is aware,
however dimly, that his opinions are not rational,
he becomes furious when they are disputed. [1]

Just a few weeks ago, the TV behind me was show-
ing scenes from the nation of Chile, South America, where
thirty-three trapped coal miners were being rescued, one
by one, after being imprisoned by a coal-mine collapse, for
sixty-nine days. As each one was removed from the rescue
capsule, he quietly and sincerely made the sign of the cross.
Did they really believe that a God "up there" or "out there"
had a hand in their rescue? Of course they did. If you were
to ask them they would tell you so. And a good percentage of Christians watching on TV, around the world, would
agree. If you argued that they were rescued by the diligent
efforts of the hundreds of workers who struggled day and
night for over two months to dig that escape hole, they
would reply that God was directing those faithful workers.
He was working through them to bring the trapped miners to the surface. I'm fairly certain no amount of rational
reflection would convince them otherwise.

One month after the successful rescue in Chile—supposedly accomplished with the help of a God "up there" or
"out there,"—another mine disaster occurred, this one in
New Zealand. Twenty-nine miners were trapped, but this

1. Russell, *Human Society,* 213.

time all twenty-nine died. Where was the Christian God? If he was there for the thirty-three, why not the twenty-nine?

Why is it that when a person looks at their own religious beliefs they seem to be blind to reality? Ask yourself this simple question: why does the human mind work like this? Why do you or I or anyone else, as a "believer," behave in such a completely irrational way? We can see the fallacy in the beliefs of other religions, but never our own.

Here is one more thought on the subject, from Bruce Hood, chair of the Cognitive Development Center in the Experimental Psychology Department at the University of Bristol, England, in his book, *Supersense.*

> Psychologists have come to the conclusion that there are at least two different systems operating when it comes to thinking and reasoning. One system is believed to be evolutionarily more ancient in terms of human development; it has been called intuitive, natural, automatic, heuristic, and implicit. It is the system we think is operating in young children before they reach school age. The second system is one that is believed to be more recent in human evolution; it permits logical reasoning but is limited by executive functions. This second reasoning system has been called conceptual-logical, analytical-rational, and explicit. It emerges much later in development and underpins the capacity of the child to perform logical, rational problem solving. When we reason about the world using these two systems, they may sometimes work in competition with each other. One might assume that those prone to the supersense and belief in

the paranormal (or supernatural) are lacking in rational thought processes, but that would be too simplistic. Studies reveal that the two systems of thinking, the intuitive and the rational, coexist in the same individuals. There are, in effect, two different ways of interpreting the world. In fact, when we measure reliance on intuition, no relationship has been found with intelligence. Intuitive people are not more stupid. They are, however, more prone to supernatural belief . . . The supersense lingers in the back of our minds, influencing our behaviors and thoughts, and our mood may play a triggering role. This explains why perfectly rational, highly educated individuals can still hold supernatural beliefs.[2]

I have no definitive answer to this question of why humans believe the unbelievable. I only ask you to recognize this phenomenon as it applies to your own faith and your own beliefs.

There is great value to be found in the teachings of Jesus, but unless the Church can confess to the mythology and folklore—delusional beliefs— that surround those teachings, fewer and fewer citizens of the twenty-first century are going to be interested in hearing them.

2. Hood, *Supersence*, 244–45.

6

Coming Clean

WHEN I was in my early teens I was a member of the Boy Scouts of America—Troop #132, First Methodist Church, Princeton, Indiana. (That was oh so long ago!) At one point our Scoutmaster was a man I'll call Mr. Edwards (not his real name). One Monday evening at troop meeting, Mr. Edwards announced a contest, "The scout who makes the most advancement between now and next summer will win a trip with me and my family to the Catskill mountains!"

Wow, what an incentive for a bunch of young boys. There was not one among us who wasn't excited over this news. It would be an adventure of unparalleled proportion for a small town boy of our age. We could hardly contain ourselves.

I was sure I could win, and I began working immediately. In the course of the next ten months I advanced several levels in the Scouting ranks, and seldom was I working on less than three or four merit badges at the same time. It became a friendly but serious competition among fellow scouts. Most of us lived near each other in the north end of town—we saw each other most every day. There was never much discussion about the competition but just below the surface, we knew it was there.

We maintained a scoreboard in the troop meeting room that allowed us to track our tangible accomplishments, but there were intangible elements to the contest as well. Mr. Edwards would also judge things like leadership, participation in troop events, and discipline.

At a meeting late in the next spring, one of my fellow scouts boldly asked Mr. Edwards when we would know the winner of the contest. Mr. Edwards paused, and then without looking up from the papers on the table he said, "I'm afraid there isn't going to be any trip to the Catskills." He then continued on with the troop business with no further explanation.

What? No trip to the Catskills? How can there be no trip to the Catskills? Had we worked our young butts off for almost a year only to hear, *"There will be no trip to the Catskills"*?

As you can imagine we were pretty upset, and several parents were upset as well. There were a few phone calls made, a few behind the scenes meetings held, and within a couple of weeks we had a new scoutmaster. Mr. Edwards had moved on. A couple of disillusioned scouts left the troop as well. As for me, I stayed and enjoyed several more years of Scouting, but this was the genesis of my total belief in the adage, "Get it in writing."

It wasn't until some time later that we (scouts) found out that Mr. Edwards had separated from his wife and was involved in a messy divorce, and that was the reason there would be no trip to the Catskills. Had Mr. Edwards explained the situation so that we would have learned of it earlier rather than later, perhaps things would have gone much better.

I do not think I am wrong in suggesting that the dilemma the Christian church finds itself in today—regarding the validity of much of the church doctrine and dogma—is quite similar to that of Scoutmaster Edwards, when he had to come clean, announce, confess, that the trip to the Catskills was not going to happen?

The church has known for several hundred years that much of the dogma and doctrine of Christianity is simply not true. It has side stepped the issue of "intellectual honesty" since the Galileo incident of the sixteenth century. With every scientific advancement, the hole has been dug deeper and deeper. Now, common knowledge makes much of what the Church proclaims nonsensical, yet to listen to the sermon delivered from just about every Christian pulpit in the world on any given Sunday, one would think that the earth is still flat, there is a dome a few hundred feet above, and God Almighty is just beyond!

For two thousand years the church has been promising forgiveness, salvation, and life ever after in a place above the sky. Comforting thoughts? Yes, but now, knowledge of the cosmos, nature, and the human condition has exposed those promises as false hope and wishful thinking. Hard to give up such beliefs? Yes, but in my opinion, if we humans are to ever mature to a more intellectual level of existence, we must begin to understand the immaturity of our former superstitious beliefs.

I remember a picture I saw some years back that, in a subtle way, speaks to the situation the church finds itself in today. In the foreground of the picture was a Cavalry officer sitting on his horse. I'll let the reader decide whether the officer was a Yankee or a Rebel, it really doesn't matter. The officer was looking out toward the viewer of the picture, but with his right hand was pointing toward the horizon, deep in the picture. Far out on that horizon was what seemed to be a cloud of dust. The caption under the picture had the officer saying, "There they go over the horizon. I must hurry and catch them, for I am their leader!"

The Cavalry officer has seemingly lost his ability to lead. His control—if indeed he ever had any—is certainly in jeopardy. I contend that the church is fast approaching this same situation.

What would happen if the church were to come clean, announce, or confess, "There really isn't a sky-god and therefore there really is no need for a savior, and, by the way, ideas of heaven and hell are simply man's longing for immortality." (Of course I wouldn't expect a pastor to speak so bluntly, but you get the message.)

Who among the clergy you know has the guts to speak so honestly from the pulpit? As was mentioned in chapter 1, their need of job security precludes them from doing so.

No matter how uncomfortable it may be, it is time for clergy to revise their worship services and in some way, and in some measure, begin to educate their congregations. Christianity can be intellectually honest and still be a vital asset to society. In my opinion, however, it must soon begin to make an honest effort to change its ways or there will be nothing of value left to save.

7

A New Concept of God

NOW THAT the ancient concept of God has been exposed as a figment of man's imagination, many scholars feel it necessary to replace "him" with a new, non-supernatural god of some kind. I don't totally agree that is necessary, however, I can understand the reluctance to simply abandon the word "God." It has been a part of human culture for, perhaps, as long as thirty thousand years.

Since humans began to puzzle over such questions as, "Where does the rain come from?" or, "What makes the wind blow?" the answer has been, some variety of god. The god explanation was the "go to" answer for all the mysteries of life. Supernaturalism was the acceptable "scientific" answer before there was such a thing as modern science. Today, no one with even a small amount of scientific knowledge would suggest that a god causes the rain to fall or the wind to blow.

Our knowledge has grown so significantly, in every area of human endeavor, that, if there were a supernatural god, that god would be, for all practical purposes, unemployed.

Many scholars today express their concept of god (note the small g) as the ultimate levels of human compassion and caring for others. In reality that's exactly what we have always expressed as the attributes of God (note the capital G). The difference, of course, is that the small "g" god is centered in the human mind, while the capital "G" God is thought of as a supernatural being, "up there" or "out there" somewhere.

When we pray to the capital "G" God, we are expecting the supernatural being to somehow intervene in the natural world and do our bidding. This is the essence of prayer, asking God to do what we ourselves cannot do.

When we pray under the concept of the small "g" god, we are focusing our thoughts on the needs of others, but with the knowledge that we must be the catalyst in making something happen. No supernatural being is going to do it for us. There has never been a prayer request of any kind answered by an imaginary supernatural God.

Theologian Paul Tillich, has described god as the Ground of all Being,[1] the life force of all living things. Biblical scholar Marcus Borg uses the word "isness" *(isness, everything that is)*, to describe god.[2]

For millions of Christians, this evolutionary change in the understanding of god has already taken place. For millions of others, the idea of any description of God other than that of a being is heresy.

The hierarchy of the church has known for centuries that it is inappropriate to think of God as a being, "up there" or "out there," but until the past few decades such knowledge has been successfully kept behind the invisible velvet curtain that hangs between the pulpit and the pews. Now, however, the silence has been broken. Christian intellectuals the

1. Tillich, *Systematic Theology*, vol 1, 64.
2. Borg, *The Heart of Christianity*, 69.

world over are beginning to speak out about this sea change in the understanding of "God" or "god." The church is faced with the inevitable problem of playing catch-up.

My purpose in writing this material is to say to the church, "Wake up, get started, don't just sit there and watch the walls crumble around you." The longer the church holds on to the ancient dogma and doctrine as literal truth, the more it makes itself irrelevant to the knowledge-based worldview of the twenty-first century.

In his book, *The American Church in Crisis*, author David Olson makes this observation about Christians and the very unpopular subject of change.

> Retreating to the safe world of the past seems enticing. Unfortunately, it does not matter what world we *want* to live in; we can only live in the world that *exists today.* The word for living in a world that no longer exists is *delusion.*[3]

His comment is certainly appropriate for the subject at hand. Millions of life-long Christians will find it hard, if not impossible, to view God in any way other than that of the "Our Father who art in Heaven" mentality, but today that view is known to be delusional. Certainly the greatest conflict between popular and academic Christianity is associated with the concept of God. God as a supernatural being has been ingrained into us since childhood. God as our protector, someone we can petition to do things we are incapable of doing, someone to look up to, someone who has all the answers to questions we cannot answer.

3. Olson, *The American Church in Crisis,* 171.

Now—just as with our childhood image of Santa—we are facing the challenge of admitting that our understanding of that supernatural God is an immature image as well. Many will find this challenge extremely difficult. But for those who are able to meet this life altering challenge, all the rest of the conflicts between popular and academic Christianity will begin to fall into place. Our image of God is the linchpin. Once that conflict is addressed the answers to many of life's mysteries suddenly come into clearer focus.

A good percentage of our Christian leadership has already crossed this divide. Now it is time for us, the people in the pews, to do the same. Christians, young and old, can broaden and strengthen their faith if they will simply speak up and ask their pastor to share with them critical information they were taught in seminary. Change can be a good thing—it need not be thought of as the end of the world!

8

Be Honest with Yourself

I KNOW I am not being very sensitive to the feelings of believers when I point out these problems associated with the popular concept of Christianity, but I want my message to be clear and unambiguous. If you find yourself disagreeing with me, please take the time to ask yourself: Why? Chances are it will be because the things I am saying are diametrically opposed to what you were taught as a child, not because they are factually wrong. Remember, in this book I am explaining to you the differences between what you and I have been taught—from the pulpit and in Sunday school all our lives— versus what our pastors have been taught in college and in seminary classes.

It so happens that I agree with the new knowledge that is being taught to our pastors, but my agreement and change of belief only came after long hours of study and many agonizing hours of reflection. My beliefs are secondary, however, to the real purpose, which is to point out the differences.

You have years and years of your life "invested" in your belief system, and perhaps, you can't bear to think that what you were taught is in error. The unmitigated truth, however, is that what I have been stating *is* factually true. The differences between popular and academic Christianity *do* exist.

And it is absolutely true that most pastors, educated in the last six decades, are aware of these differences.

Be honest with yourself, there is no rational reason to believe the myth and folklore of the Bible to be true, unless you can produce evidence that refutes the Christian professionals in our colleges and seminaries, and the research that suggests otherwise. Simply believing what you have always believed for no other reason than that it is what you have always believed is illogical and naive.

Furthermore there is no legitimate reason for the church to continue withholding such information from the laity. The longer the church maintains the charade, the more foolish it looks. Religions always evolve and Christianity must evolve also, or it will die.

We cannot continue to appeal to a new generation that is being taught a more intellectually honest understanding of religion, by insisting that the ancient beliefs are the ultimate truth for all ages. It is an insult to the intelligence of the very people the church is seeking to attract.

I felt the same way you do right now, when at the age of fifty-six I first began reading and studying what seemed to me to be pure heresy. If I remember right the first book I read—recommended to me by a retired pastor friend—was, *Meeting Jesus Again for the First Time* by Marcus Borg. I became intrigued, and went on to read other Christian scholars who were "coming out" (as it were) about the knowledge that the church had been keeping hidden for the past three hundred years and—for the most part—is still hiding. The more I read the more anxious I became. I began to talk to pastor friends about these things. Reluctantly—to some extent—most of them agreed with the information I was reading. Most confided that they had, indeed, been exposed to the same information in their seminary years, but did not feel they could pass such information on to their congregations without suffering dire consequences: loss of membership, revenue, even their job.

Obviously there are many other areas of liturgy, creed and ritual that must be changed once the ten I have mentioned are redefined, i.e., prayer, confession, hymns, communion, invocation, and worship. There are very few resources today for those who wish to move toward a more honest and intellectual Christian worship service. Innovative Christians who desire to see the church survive must help develop them. One good source of intellectually honest liturgy for the church is the website maintained by The Center for Progressive Christianity (http://www.tcpc. org). This organization has steadily grown over the past several years and is slowly becoming a valuable resource to those for whom organized religion has become ineffectual, irrelevant, or repressive.

I have no precise plan of how to go about making the changes I have suggested. There are others who are better qualified to perform that task. My goal is to awaken the church and the laity to the need for the change. The change, in my opinion, will only come when there is a critical mass of informed lay men and women, large enough to demand that the church teach and preach to the people in the pews, the same intellectually honest doctrine being taught in our colleges and seminaries. Let's hope that happens soon.

9

With Knowledge Comes Change

FOR THE past three thousand years, the Abrahamic religions (Judaism, Christianity, and Islam) have professed a belief in a god described as a supernatural being, out there or up there—somewhere separate and distinctly apart from this world. A god who is all knowing, all-powerful, and ever present. A god who can be prayed to and placated. A god who from time to time reaches down and imposes his will upon the world and/or individuals. Today that description of God is, both morally and intellectually bankrupt.

In the intellectual worldview of the twenty-first century, belief in such a god is relegated to those who are unwilling to ask questions or are uninterested in exploring the history of religion and God. There are, perhaps, three billion people—half the population of the earth—who fit this category.

There is no requirement that we accept any new ideas, but can we at least look? Are we willing to explore? Can we open our minds to the possibility that this might be worth some thought? Unfortunately, one of the problems with our world today is that too many human minds are closed. We imagine ourselves to know everything we need to know on the subject of God.

We are willing to explore other things,

- New developments in science,
- New theories in economics,
- New approaches in education,
- New frontiers in outer space.

Yet when we speak of religion, many of us—most of us perhaps—are unwilling to explore any new ideas at all. To question is blasphemy, we say. To question is unallowable, we say. And in many cases, it is punishable by excommunication, even death.

But change has always been a part of life.

Actress Marlene Dietrich was a popular film star of the twentieth century. Her career spanned sixty-one years, from 1919 to 1980. Ms Dietrich died in 1992. There is a story told about her that I cannot verify, but I will use it to make a point. The story goes that in 1936, Ms Dietrich was making a movie titled *The Garden of Allah*. It is told she had a favorite cameraman on the movie set who (she thought) seemed to take all her shots with just the right lighting and just the right angles to bring out her best features.

Then the story goes that some twenty years later on yet another movie set, she came across that same cameraman—where he had been for twenty years, I don't know. Ms Dietrich, recalling this cameraman's expertise, insisted that the director allow him to do all of her film shots. Which he did.

One afternoon a few days later, while viewing the film of that day's shooting, Ms Dietrich confided in the cameraman, "I don't know," she said, "they just don't seem the same as they did before. The pictures look different for some reason." The cameraman is said to have replied, very politely . . . "Well you know Marlene darling, my camera is twenty years older!"

Boy, I wish I could think that fast! I would have probably said something stupid, like, "Well, what do you expect? Look at those 'crows feet' you've got around your eyes, and those wrinkles on your forehead, and what about that 'turkey neck' thing you've got going on there."

But this guy is cool . . . "Well you know my camera is twenty years older!"

This guy could be the patron saint of every man who has ever been asked the question . . . "Honey, does this dress make me look too heavy?"

Well, whether the difference was the age of the camera or the age of the actress is immaterial. The point here is: everything changes over time.

If things didn't change, instead of using a modern-day cell phone to communicate with our friends and relatives, we might still be using the telegraph machine or the pony express. Or, instead of driving to the store in a comfortable air-conditioned car, we might be riding a wagon or buggy, pulled by a horse or mule.

Everything changes over time . . . even religion. If religion didn't change over time, we might still be making burnt sacrifices on our church alters on Sunday mornings. Or we might still believe that God resided on his throne just a few hundred feet up in the air, just beyond the blue canopy that hangs over the flat earth.

This is the nature of all religions, and all of life. For thousands of years, as humans have gained wisdom and knowledge, everything around us has changed, even our religions, even our concepts of God.

Ten thousand years ago people believed in many gods and goddesses. Each god or goddess was thought to have control over a particular element of nature. People prayed to these gods and goddesses and offered them sacrifices to seek their favor and protection.

Then, four thousand years ago the world began to move through what has been called the First Axial Period, during which some—but not all—religions began to combine the powers of all their gods and goddesses into one supreme god. A move that was both religious and political. The first recorded attempt to make such a move occurred in Mesopotamia around the beginning of the second millennium BCE when the god Marduk was the head of the Mesopotamian pantheon of gods. The movement lasted only a short time.

The second occurrence of a move toward monotheism took place in Egypt, in the fourteenth century BCE, under the reign of the pharaoh known as Amenhotep IV. This new young pharaoh elevated his favorite god, Aten to the position of "the one and only god." It was said of this god Aten that he "decreed life" and "created the earth." Amenhotep IV had the temples of all the other gods erased from the face of the earth and their priesthoods were done away with. But this attempt at monotheism failed as well and Aten eventually fell from grace and was replaced by still other gods.

The third attempt at worshiping a single god occurred in the seventh century BCE in Israel, under the reign of King Josiah. Many Christians are unaware that prior to this time the Israelites worshiped several gods. But King Josiah, like pharaoh Amenhotep IV, was interested in consolidating the powers into the hands of one god, Yahweh. The story of how King Josiah went about this task can be found in 2 Kings. It is a gruesome and bloodthirsty story.

This new supreme god of the Israelites had one primary purpose: to watch over and protect the Hebrew nation. At that time, Yahweh was the tribal god of the Hebrews, and the Hebrews only.

Then two thousand years ago that concept of god changed yet again when the Christians made Yahweh into a personal god for all people of all nations, Jew and Gentile alike.

Today, as I have tried to point out in this book, we are in the midst of yet another ecclesiastical change, one that began some 250 to 300 years ago—a change that moves our understanding of God from a supernatural being, up there or out there, to a god within, a change that reinterprets our concept of God from being the creator of life, to being the essence of life.

Most of us are uncomfortable with change, especially when it affects our religious beliefs. To make such changes takes many people out of their comfort zone, and yet—as I have just described—change has been a vital part of our religion throughout history. That which does not change as knowledge increases, soon becomes irrelevant.

My thirty-year career as a supervisor and manager in the aerospace industry occurred during the most traumatic period of change in industrial operating systems since the beginning of the industrial era. It was a time during which every operating system in the industrial arena—financial, planning, production, production control, inventory control, purchasing, human resources, customer service, maintenance, and others—were converted from manual to computerized systems. This drastic revolution affected every discipline in the industrial world. It changed people's daily lives in ways they could never have imagined. Every aspect of every process underwent change.

The change did not happen overnight. It was gradual, over a period of several years. First one discipline would change, then another, and another. As new computer software was written and older software was updated and replaced, more change was implemented. No one, no department, no industry was immune. Change became the only constant. There was no choice. To remain competitive, companies around the world were compelled to change.

But as the reader might imagine, this change was not always met with enthusiasm. As with any change which involves humans, there was resistance. The old manual systems were working. Many people, including some supervisors and managers, saw no reason to change. In fact, many of the supervisors and managers had helped install or improve upon the older manual systems and were therefore reluctant to see them discarded. They understood the workings of the manual systems and with that understanding came power—another reason to resist the change to a new and unknown system.

Eventually, however, most everyone saw the wisdom in making the changes and the implementation process continued forward. Those who would not or could not bring themselves to change were simply relegated to the fringes of the organization or let go altogether. Today, computerized operating systems are the norm. No major company could exist without them.

This picture of industrial change is but a foreshadow of what I see for the future of the church. Change is inevitable. The church cannot continue to keep its constituents in darkness. The differences between popular and academic Christianity have been exposed. Our colleges and seminaries are speaking and teaching an understanding of the Christian faith that is entirely foreign to the people in the pews. Of course there will be resistance, but just as with those who would not or could not change in industry, those who cannot or will not change within the church will find themselves on the fringes among the uninformed and uneducated.

The church cannot grow—or even survive—if it continues to preach a doctrine, which it knows to be antiquated, delusional, and false.

∽

For quite some time, I have struggled with the question of how to end this book, because, for me, it is not an ending—it is but another data point along my journey to a better understanding of religion. A point at which I have the opportunity to share some of what I have already discovered with you, the reader.

I suspect that most people will never have a traumatic experience; such as I had (chapter 1), that prompts them to undertake an extensive study of their beliefs. Certainly I am not happy to have had the disturbing experience, but the ensuing study of gods and religion has been rewarding beyond my wildest imagination. My studies have opened my eyes to a world that is much more understandable than the world of folklore, magic, miracles, and myth, which were the makeup of my former Christian belief system. I hope the reader will be inquisitive enough to pursue further reading on these matters. There is no doubt in my mind that the rewards will be great.

I am optimistic that as our universities and seminaries continue producing more and more citizens with an intellectually honest understanding of religion, the church will be compelled to "come clean" regarding its secretive past. I am aware of a few churches where this revelation is already in process.

In her book, *With or Without God*, Rev. Gretta Vosper—speaking of the church— states:[1]

> Its role as spiritual leader is diminishing as a result of its inability to share the truth it knows instead of the 'Truth' it pretends to know. Harsh? So has been the effect on many who fail to 'believe' the Truth presented by the church but who passionately seek truth for living. This truth must be explored within the church, spoken in the church, and celebrated in the church. The church needs to be the place where this happens.

I would encourage the reader to investigate further the information I have provided herein. Talk to your pastor. Ask him or her if this material was present during his or her seminary training. Begin a dialog about how this information can be infused into the education of the people in the

---

1. Vosper. *With or Without*, 18.

pews in your church. Christianity will be stronger when we can, at last, be honest with each other.

Peace.
BEB

Bibliography

Adler, Mortimer. *Truth in Religion*. New York: Macmillan, 1990.

Allen, Grant. *The Evolution of the Idea of God*. Escondido, CA: The Book Tree, 2000.

Allport, Gordon. *The Individual and His Religion*. New York: Macmillan, 1950.

Armstrong, Karen. *A History of God*. New York: Ballantine, 1993.

———. *In the Beginning*. New York: Alfred A. Knopf, 1996.

Barnes, Harry E., *An Intellectual and Cultural History of the Western World*. 3rd rev. ed. Vol. 1. New York: Dover, 1965.

Bass, Diana Butler. *Christianity for the Rest of Us*. New York: HarperCollins, 2006.

Battle, John A. "Charles Hodge, Inspiration, Textual Criticism, and the Princeton Doctrine of Scripture," The Christian Observer, No pages, Online: http://christianobserver.org/charles-hodge-inspiration-testual-criticism-and-the-princeton-doctrine-of-scripture/.

Benson, Andrew. *The Origins of Christianity and the Bible*. Clovis, CA: Prudential, 1997.

Blood, Barry. *Christian Dogma*. Xulon, 2004.

Borg, Marcus J. *God in 2000*. Harrisburg: Morehouse, 2000.

———. *Meeting Jesus Again for the First Time*. San Francisco: HarperSanFrancisco, 1995.

———. *The God We Never Knew*. San Francisco: HarperSanFrancisco, 1998.

———. *The Heart of Christianity*. San Francisco: HarperSanFrancisco, 2003.

Bowker, John, *God : A Brief History*. New York: DK, 2002.

Bracken, Joseph A. *What Are They Saying About the Trinity?* New York: Paulist, 1979.

Cox, Harvey. *Religion in the Secular City.* New York: Simon and Schuster, 1984.

————. *The Future of Faith.* New York: HarperOne, 2009.

Crossan, John Dominic. *The Historical Jesus.* New York: HarperCollins, 1992.

Cupitt, Don. *After God.* New York: BasicBooks, 1997.

————. *Reforming Christianity.* Santa Rosa, CA: Polebridge, 2001.

Draina, C. "Holy Trinity." *New Catholic Encyclopedia,* 2nd ed. vol. 14, Farmington Hills: Gale, 2003.

Ehrman, Bart. *God's Problem.* New York: HarperOne, 2008.

————. *Jesus, Interrupted.* New York: HarperOne, 2009.

————. *Misquoting Jesus.* San Francisco: HarperSanFrancisco, 2005.

Frazer, James G. *The Golden Bough.* New York: Avenel Books, 1981.

Freud, Sigmund. *The Future of an Illusion.* New York: W. W. Norton, 1961.

Friedman, Richard E. *Who Wrote the Bible.* New York: HarperCollins, 1989.

Funk, Robert W. *Honest to Jesus.* San Francisco: HarperSanFrancisco, 1996.

Geering, Lloyd. *Christianity Without God.* Santa Rosa: Polebridge, 2002.

Goff, Vernon G. *Making God Talk Make Sense.* Lincoln, NE: Dageforde, 2001.

Good, Jack. *The Dishonest Church.* Haworth, NJ: St. Johann, 2008.

Graves, Kersey. *The World's Sixteen Crucified Saviors.* New York: Cosimo, 2007.

Greenberg, Gary. *101 Myths of the Bible.* Naperville, IL: Sourcebooks, 2002.

Fortman, Edmund J. *The Triune God.* Eugene: Wipf and Stock, 1999.

Hadden, Jeffrey. *Religion in Radical Transition.* Chicago: Aldine, 1971.

Halloway, Richard. *Doubts and Loves.* Edinburgh: Canongate, 2001.

————. *Godless Morality.* Edinburgh: Canongate, 1999.

Helms, Randel *Who Wrote the Gospels.* Altadena, CA: Millennium Press, 1996.

Hood, Bruce M. *Supersense.* San Francisco: HarperCollins, 2009.

Hopfe, Lewis M. *Religions of the World.* New York: Macmillan, 1987.

Keck, Leander E. *A Future for the Historical Jesus.* Nashville: Abingdon, 1971.

LaCugna, C. M. *"Trinity."* Encyclopedia of Religion, Vol. 14, Farmington Hills, MI: Macmillan, 2005.

Laughlin, Paul Alan. *Remedial Christianity.* Santa Rosa: Polebridge, 2000.

Lohse, Bernhard. *A Short History of Christian Doctrine.* Minneapolis: Fortress, 1966.

Magee, Dr Michael D. *The Hidden Jesus.* United Kingdom: Ask Why!, 1997.

Mead, Loren B. *Five Challenges for the Once and Future Church,* Herndon, VA: Alban Institute, 1996.

Olsen, David T. *The American Church in Crisis.* Grand Rapids, MI: Zondervan, 2008.

Overstreet. *The Mature Mind.* New York: Franklin Watts, 1959.

Paine, Thomas. *The Age of Reason.* Amherst, NY: Prometheus, 1984.

Pelikan, Jaroslav. *Jesus Through the Centuries.* Binghamton, NY: Yale University, 1985.

Pew Research. "Many Americans Uneasy with Mix of Religion and Politics." Sec. IV, No pages. Online: http://pewforum.org/Politics-and-Elections/Many-Americans-Uneasy-with-Mix-of-Religion-and-Politics.aspx#4.

Ranke-Heinemann, Uta. *Putting Away Childish Things.* New York: HarperCollins, 1995.

Robinson, John A. T. *Honest to God.* Philadelphia: Westminster, 1963.
———. *The Human Face of God.* Philadelphia: Westminster, 1973.

Russell, Bertrand. *Human Society in Ethics and Politics.* New York: Routledge, 1992.

Spong, John Shelby. *A New Christianity for a New World.* San Francisco: HarperSanFrancisco, 2001.
———. *Eternal Life: A New Vision.* New York: HarperCollins, 2009.
———. *Jesus for the Non-Religious.* San Francisco: HarperSanFrancisco, 2007.
———. *Rescuing the Bible from Fundamentalism.* San Francisco: HarperSanFrancisco, 1992.
———. *Why Christianity Must Change or Die.* San Francisco: HarperSanFrancisco, 1999.

Stenger, Victor J. *God, The failed Hypothesis.* Amherst: Prometheus, 2007.

Taussig, Hal. *A New Spiritual Home.* Santa Rosa, CA: Polebridge, 2006.

Tillich, Paul. *Systematic Theology,* Vol. 1. Chicago: University of Chicago, 1973.

———. *The Shaking of the Foundations.* New York: C. Scribner's Sons, 1948.

Unknown. *"Trinity."* Encyclopedia Britannica, vol. 11, Chicago: Britannica, 2005.

Vosper, Gretta. *With or Without God.* Toronto: HarperCollins, 2008.

Walsch, Neale Donald. *What God Wants.* New York: Atria, 2005.

Wright, Robert. *The Evolution of God.* New York: Back Bay, 2010.

www.ingramcontent.com/pod-product-compliance
Lightning Source LLC
Chambersburg PA
CBHW060414090426
42734CB00011B/2319